MARY,
Woman of Nazareth

Biblical and Theological Perspectives

Edited with an Introduction by
Doris Donnelly

PAULIST PRESS
New York/Mahwah

Acknowledgments
Dr. Elizabeth A. Johnson's article, "Mary and the Female Face of God," originally appeared in *Theological Studies* (September, 1989) and is reprinted with permission. Dr. Johnson's article, "Mary in Praxis-Oriented Theology," a contribution to the Festschrift for René Laurentin, is also reprinted with permission.

Library of Congress Cataloging-in-Publication Data

Mary, woman of Nazareth: biblical and theological perspectives/edited with an
  introduction by Doris Donnelly.
       p.   cm.
    Includes bibliographical references.
    ISBN 0-8091-3109-9
    1. Mary, Blessed Virgin, Saint—Theology.   I. Donnelly, Doris.
  BT613.M385 1990
  232.91—dc20   89-36862
                                                                   CIP

Published by Paulist Press
997 Macarthur Blvd.
Mahwah, N.J. 07430

Printed and bound in the United States of America

TABLE OF CONTENTS

Foreword

In response to the Marian Year declared by Pope John Paul II, the Center for Spirituality at Saint Mary's College extended an invitation to renowned scholars in Marian studies and asked them to push forward the frontiers of this important subject in Christian life and literature. From June 12 to June 16, 1988, specialists in scripture, theology, ecumenism, evangelism, peace studies, the arts and humanities gathered on Saint Mary's campus in South Bend.

Few events in the history of our college have been better suited to reflect the reason for our existence than this symposium. Our perduring interest in scholarship, especially when it involves the namesake of our school, as well as our commitment to in-depth probing of subjects relating to women's spiritual development, marked these few days as a particularly appropriate expression of our mission in education.

This volume is our way of extending the influence of the Mary symposium to as wide an audience as possible. I am grateful to the authors of the papers and to the enthusiastic symposium participants. Most of all, however, I am grateful to Dr. Doris Donnelly who conceived the idea for the symposium, planned and organized it, and edited the publication of this outstanding volume.

William A. Hickey, Ph.D.
President, Saint Mary's College
Notre Dame, Indiana

Introduction

Doris Donnelly

One of the events that occupied the attention of Christians from the fifth century onward was the dormition of Mary. Literally, the phrase "dormition of the Virgin" means the falling asleep of the Virgin, and in keeping with the early understanding of death as sleep, it figuratively referred to Mary's last days on earth.

I do not think I would be overstating the case if I were to refer to the period between the Second Vatican Council and the mid-1980's as another dormition of the Virgin. Mary's popularity as well as theological interest in her had waned significantly. For a time she appeared to be slumbering in the collective unconscious of the Christian community.

The gradual reemergence of Mary as a preeminent member of the church began to take formidable shape and scope in the last few years. Because the resurfacing was happening in the context of a balanced theology and piety which attended to scriptural, patristic and biblical roots as well as to pastoral and ecumenical implications, it was particular cause for celebration. It was also the primary impetus for gathering a community of scholars to share their significant research with the wider community.

If it seemed necessary, even urgent, to coordinate the gains made in Marian studies, it also appeared especially fitting that Saint Mary's College should be the place for the dialogue and consolidation. After all, a conference at Saint Mary's College during the Marian Year was almost irresistible!

3

We were aware, however, that a symposium on Mary and this subsequent book would be only as good as their contributors, and we were fortunate that so many distinguished scholars accepted our invitation to be part of a convocation at Saint Mary's in mid-June 1988. The rigorous, insightful and often pioneering work of these men and women honored their subject as much as it honored our institution.

Anne Carr's keynote essay sets the stage for us: Mary is a model of faith for all Christians, male and female. With *Redemptoris Mater,* the encyclical of John Paul II on Mary in the background, Sister Carr guides us to some new thinking and new imaging of Mary.

Systematic theologian Elizabeth Johnson is responsible for two major essays. In the first, she helps us disconnect Mary from direct salvific and sanctifying roles which more accurately belong to God but which have attached themselves to Mary over the centuries. Once the divestment is completed, Sister Johnson restructures a Marian theology by taking into account third world and praxis oriented themes.

The biblical field is well represented by Donald Senior, Pheme Perkins and Richard Sklba. Father Senior and Professor Perkins attend to New Testament considerations of Mary while Bishop Sklba focuses on the Old Testament theme of the *'anawim* and its application to Mary.

The important connection between Mary and justice, alluded to by all conference speakers, is the specific point of concentration for Carol Frances Jegen and Virgilio Elizondo. Sister Jegen provides perspective on Mary's role in the worldwide struggle for justice and peace while Father Elizondo specifies the Guadalupe phenomenon as a focus for evangelization.

John Shinners closes these pages with a study of some of the important historical moments in the development of the cult of Mary.

In addition to my gratitude to the authors of these provocative essays, it is also true that any effort at writing that finds its way into print owes a great deal to a supporting cast. At the conference itself, the assistance of Dr. Loretta Jancoski was inestimable, and she and I both owe much to our daughters Kathleen Jancoski and Peggy Donnelly for the many tasks they performed with zest and enthusiasm. The Sisters of the Holy Cross provided superb hospitality at Regina Hall, and Sister Francis Rose, CSC, in her typically quiet way, found ways that exceeded all expectations to support the conference. Judy Smith, an accomplished writer and editor, made my task of editing a pleasure. And the president of Saint Mary's College, Dr. William Hickey, recognized the symposium as an idea whose time had come and encouraged it unfailingly from its embryonic origins to completion.

The generosity and talent of so many made this project a joy which I am delighted to share with you.

South Bend, IN
December 8, 1988

Mary: Model of Faith

Anne Carr

In March 1987 Pope John Paul II issued his sixth encyclical, *Redemptoris Mater,* one of several recent actions on the part of the institutional church which makes a reconsideration of Mary especially timely. He declared the period from Pentecost 1987 until the feast of the Assumption 1988 a Marian Year, a time of special reflection on and renewal of devotion to Mary, the mother of Jesus.[1] In one of her oldest titles, *Theotokos,* Mary is called the very mother of God, venerated in the east as in the west. This is an ecumenical bond of no small importance to the pope as he refers to both the coming of Christianity to Russia one thousand years ago and the coming of the third millennium of Christianity itself (*RM* 3, 31, 33, 50). It is in Mary, the encyclical further notes, that women especially are to find "the secret of living their femininity with dignity and of achieving their own true advancement" (*RM* 46).

More recently, the United States bishops released the first draft of their pastoral response to women's concerns for church and society, *Partners in the Mystery of Redemption.*[2] They indicate that "Mary stands as a model for all Christians of what it means to be a partner with God in the work of salvation" even as she "is a special symbol for women" (*PMR* 239–40). These official documents encourage us to explore the meaning of Mary in our lives as Christians today, to ask what she has meant in the past and what she can mean for us today and in the future. How is it that we can speak of Mary as a model of faith

7

for all Christians? And how is it that she is a special model for women?

1. THE CAUTIONS OF THE PAST

History cautions us to take special care in several areas. First there is the troubling image of women that many past depictions of Mary conveyed. As the bishops of the United States note, many women today are unhappy with representations that propose Mary as a model of "passivity and submission to male authority, a woman valued chiefly for her virginity and maternity, a woman confined to domestic and familial roles" (*PMR* 242). Moreover they point out that sometimes Mary has been so exalted because of her special privileges that she seems beyond imitation by ordinary women (*PMR* 242). Some women writers have found in Mary's virginity and motherhood an inimitable double bind; they object to her historical representations as encouraging only docility, humility, and self-effacement as the particular virtues for women.[3] For these analysts, the history of Marian devotion, rich and beautiful as it may be, might have some unintended but prophetic meaning for the future coming-to-be of women. For Mary Daly, Mary may be seen as a figure of authentic female autonomy.[4] Or it may be, as Marina Warner suggests, that Marian devotion is empty of moral significance today, especially for contemporary women who are struggling to realize their full personhood.[5] At the very least, we must maintain what novelist Mary Gordon has called a "forgiving vigilance" with regard to Marian tradition.[6] Mary is important as a singular female figure in the horizon of historic Christianity, but her image as a woman has been used in ways that warrant critical scrutiny.

History also cautions against the proliferation of Marian devotions that seemed to make Mary of equal importance with Jesus Christ or made her a divine figure or displaced the central liturgy of eucharist and sacraments by exaggerated focus on Mary in novenas, rosary, or pilgrimage. Both Luther and Calvin had praise for Mary but objected to the inflation of her importance. Festivals in her honor sometimes distracted Christians from biblically based Christ-centered and God-centered worship and attitudes.[7] Today critics point out that the scriptural sources contain even less information about the "historical Mary" than about the historical Jesus. And most of what the scriptures record is theological reflection by the early Christian communities after Jesus' resurrection.[8] While the beginnings of the symbolic rendering of Mary may already be discerned in the New Testament, especially in the infancy narratives of Matthew and Luke and in the fourth gospel, that symbolic growth must be kept in check theologically by the insistence that in the Christian perspective there is only one mediator, Jesus Christ. The recent papal document maintains that insistence, especially as it reiterates the teaching of Vatican Council II in chapter eight of *Lumen Gentium* (*RM* 22, 38). Mary is not equal to Christ in the Christian scheme and she is not God.[9]

The question of Marian apparitions is also troubling. The period from 1850 to 1950 is often called the Marian age because of the definitions by the papacy of the two dogmas of the immaculate conception in 1854 and the assumption of Mary in 1950. These definitions testify to the revival of Marian piety that surrounded the many reported apparitions of the Virgin in southern and western Europe in the nineteenth and early twentieth centuries, some of which gained widespread fame and church approval (e.g. Paris in 1830, La Salette in 1846, Lourdes in 1858, Fatima in 1917 and others).[10] These apparitions aroused great hopes and fears, and their sites eventually attracted pilgrims from all walks of life. The resulting images of Mary paradoxically divinized her yet never stressed her active cooperation in Christ's redemption. (At La Salette she is reported to have said, "I gave you six days' work. I have reserved the seventh for myself," words that identify her with God.) Her privileges as intermediary were given to her as a pure and passive vessel. One historian notes that the apparitions never carried a message of social transformation or the overcoming of exploitation and oppression. "The political direction they augured was always backward rather than forward: in favor of

kings and the old social order and fearful of change."[11] The
apparitions were attached to messages of aggressive anti-com-
munism and cold war and (in several recent, unapproved but
popular instances) to defense of a pre-Vatican II faith.

Thus the Mary symbol has encouraged passive and submissive roles for women, issued in a proliferation of devotions that
exceeded scriptural and theological boundaries, and encouraged reactionary views of faith and the social order. And yet it is
clear that the symbol of Mary has also meant something more.
Over the centuries, both women and men have turned to Mary,
recognizing in her image something beautiful and powerful
that filled important religious and Christian needs. A prayer
from the late third century reads: "We fly to thy patronage, O
holy mother of God. Despise not our petitions in our necessities; deliver us from all dangers, O glorious and blessed Virgin."[12] A glance at the history of Marian art and devotion
suggests the power of her symbol in its many transformations in
different times and places: she is black, brown, yellow, and
white, depending on the ethnic context. She is peasant and
queen, simple Jewish girl, stately figure of wisdom, happy
young mother, anguished and grieving widow, or liberated
leader and woman of courage, depending on the popular or
national situation.[13] Who is this woman whom we all associate
(for better or worse) with our own mothers, or with wives or
daughters or sisters or other important women in our lives?
Who is this Mary? And how can we talk of her today as a model
of faith? What is her peculiar power as an important religious
symbol within the Christian horizon?

2. RECENT FEMINIST DISCUSSION

Over the last decade, Christian women (and some feminist
men) have begun to look at Mary with new eyes. After all, she is
one of the few female figures in our religious history and surely
the most important.[14] Although Elisabeth Moltmann Wendel
holds that the figure of the Magdalene is significant for women
today, especially as she represents a model of friendship and

apostleship (rather than motherhood) that is witnessed in the scriptures and in the history of art and iconography,[15] the centrality of Mary the Mother of Jesus seems inarguable. One scholar, Donal Flanagan, is especially critical of traditional mariology as the creation of men who put Mary on a pedestal as the good virgin and mother, contrasting her with the sinful Eve as the symbol of all ordinary women.[16] This contrast between Mary and Eve is unlike the parallel Christ/Adam distinction in its negative effects for women. Flanagan points out that the use of Mary must be subjected to theological as well as feminist criticism if it is to be regenerated for Christians today.

One of these feminist critics, Joan Chamberlain Engelsman, has shown how Mary came to embody all the characteristics of the biblical figure of *Wisdom* over the course of history,[17] while Rosemary Radford Ruether argues that Mary is a symbol of the feminine face of the *church*, a liberated humanity.[18] Another insightful view is expressed by Elisabeth Schüssler Fiorenza. She claims that over the centuries Mary came to embody the feminine dimension of the biblical God.[19] As the figure of God became more transcendent, more distant in Christian understanding, Mary became more important as a religious figure symbolizing divine immanence. Because God was imaged as a male, a stern judge, a warrior, an omnipotent ruler, king, or tyrant, or a benevolent but demanding father, the characteristics of tenderness, mercy, strength, and compassion of the God of the Bible were displaced by popular devotion onto the figure of Mary. Recently, feminist theologians have sought to develop new models and metaphors for God or for the God-human relation, as in Sallie McFague's provocative depictions for a nuclear and ecological age: God as mother, lover, friend.[20] As language for God becomes more inclusive and various within the Christian community, and as it becomes clear in our worship and our theology that God transcends sexuality but is the source of all the characteristics of both sexes, what happens to Mary? Is she in fact diminished by new perceptions of the many cosmic and personal metaphors for the incomprehensible God of mystery?[21]

3. BIBLICAL CRITICISM

Recent discussions by scripture scholars have certainly cautioned us about how little can be known with any certainty about the "historical Mary." John McKenzie, drawing on the scholarship of Raymond Brown, Joseph Fitzmyer, and others, put the matter quite baldly: "No doubt historical and biblical criticism ha[ve] an iconoclastic effect upon Mariology."[22] In McKenzie's summary of the New Testament evidence as an historical and theological source, he claims that there is no historical basis for the beliefs in the immaculate conception or the assumption of Mary, nor for belief in her as the mediatrix of all grace. The infancy narratives of Matthew and Luke are the only sources for belief in the virginal conception of Jesus, as they are for the name of Joseph, and for the birth of Jesus at Bethlehem. Like the Cana and Calvary stories in the gospel of John, they are complex theological constructions which are quite distinct from the rest of Matthew and Luke and are apparently unknown to the other New Testament writers. Nor do the texts afford any historical basis for belief in the perpetual virginity or sinlessness of Mary.[23]

McKenzie is clear that he is speaking only of the New Testament as a critical historical source. The question of tradition is another matter, although he allows that biblical criticism is no kinder to tradition itself. He disagrees with Brown and his ecumenical team that there is basis in the New Testament for referring to Mary as the ideal disciple.[24] Moreover, as McKenzie lines up the New Testament exegetical facts about Mary, he notes the harshness of Jesus toward his physical family, including his mother, in favor of the new spiritual family that he preaches and brings to people (Mk 3:21, 31–35). The one positive suggestion that emerges is that, while Mark and Matthew do not present Mary as a disciple, Luke's gospel (2:19, 51) may indicate the beginnings of discipleship, and Acts (1:14) expressly places her in the company of believers who receive the Holy Spirit at Pentecost. McKenzie argues that "faith in the Mary of traditional Christian devotion is faith in something which is not true."[25] Not historically true, that is. This is not to say that Marian tradition does not communicate a deep symbolic truth, granted the corrective surgery that critical exegesis performs. I would hold that symbolic truth is more, not less, than truth that can be historically verified. This symbolic truth —perhaps Catholics would, in retrospect, call it tradition—is subject to the criticism of contemporary biblical scholarship and held in check by it, but it enables us to suggest the new and powerful meanings that Mary holds for Christians today.

4. THEOLOGICAL REFLECTIONS

Critical biblical study is not the only razor that has been applied to traditional understandings of Mary. Recent theological discussions as well have underscored the absolute centrality of Jesus for Christian understanding, the dual concern of Jesus for both God and human beings, and the central significance of Jesus' whole life as it culminates in his death and resurrection. Contemporary christological thought, beginning with Pannenberg, worked out in some of Rahner's later essays, and most fully developed in Schillebeeckx's massive analyses in *Jesus* and *Christ*, has stressed the importance today of following the New Testament historical perspectives (the synoptic gospels rather than John) in understanding Jesus.[26] In this framework, variously called an ascending christology or christology "from below," emphasis is placed on the whole of Jesus' life and ministry, especially on his death and resurrection. As Pannenberg and the later Schillebeeckx see it, the idea of the incarnation, the point of departure of John's gospel (and for the infancy narratives of Matthew and Luke which refer to Mary) is in fact the point of arrival for the more historically genetic accounts which allow us to trace something of the experience of Jesus in history.[27] As Rahner sees it, an ascending christology fills out historically and corrects the equally necessary descending christology of the incarnation.[28] Faith in the incarnation as it is expressed in a descending christology is a statement of praise and worship, a conclusion of faith rather than a beginning. In our historically conscious age, the work of these theologians on what little can be known of the historical path of Jesus and early

Christianity satisfies a certain need to know how Christian belief came to be.[29]

As Elizabeth Johnson has shown, the earlier discussions of Mary by Rahner and Schillebeeckx, cast in the horizon of a descending Christology (from "God's point of view") like an earlier mariology generally, came close to divinizing Mary as a co-principle of redemption.[30] The later christological points of view of these theologians, cast now more historically "from below" and in the light of human experience, alter their perspectives on Mary. Mary would be seen, according to the few references to her in the synoptic gospels (excluding the infancy narratives), as a very human figure who had doubts and hesitations, who perhaps requested that Jesus stop his itinerant preaching and attend to his duties in the patriarchal family, and who came to faith with the other disciples after Jesus' death and resurrection. This very human Mary, who moved from unbelief to belief, who experienced the concern of a mother over her son's unorthodox activities, especially as he ran afoul of the religious and political authorities, and who, with the disciples, knew anguish at his death—this Mary can indeed serve as a model of faith for all Christians.[31]

At the Second Vatican Council, the council fathers made a decision of major importance when they voted, by a narrow margin, to include discussion of Mary in the document on the church, *Lumen Gentium*.[32] Later, when the council's *Constitution on the Church* was promulgated, Pope Paul VI declared Mary the mother of the church. There have been criticisms of the traditional depiction of Mary in the council statement,[33] just as one may criticize the rather literal statement of traditional mariology, the androcentrism, and the stereotypical view of women in Pope John Paul II's *Redemptoris Mater* (7–23, 46). But the council struck a right note in placing Mary in relation to Christ in the mystery of the church. The pope's recent letter is equally firm in reiterating the council's affirmation of Mary in the context of Christ and the church. But further, in this letter, there is the important suggestion of Mary's presence in the pilgrim church as she is a model of faith for the whole church (5, 6, 16, 25, 29, 37, 42, 44, 47).

5. MARY AS MODEL OF FAITH

As we go about revisioning the long tradition about Mary in art and music, devotion and theology, it may seem that the narrow limits set by critical exegesis severely cramp any creative possibilities. But I propose that they do not. In fact, as McKenzie himself suggests, Christian women (and men) may be about the task of creating a new mariology in seeing Mary precisely as a human figure, imperfect, growing in faith, moving from unbelief to belief in the struggle of her life. The pope's recent letter several times repeats the phrase "journey of faith" in referring to Mary's life and her place in the pilgrim church (5, 16, 25, 28). By this he means her own historical movement to faith as well as her place in our lives as Christians, as members of Christ in the church. She symbolizes, for the tradition, both the path of faith and the fruition of Christian life (24, 37, 42, 44, 47, 49). She has become, as Elizabeth Johnson has suggested, that corporate personality who embodies symbolically the past, present, and future of Christian life.[34] Beyond the narrow confines of an individual, historical life, she has become, over the course of centuries, a more-than-human figure. She is at once that little-known historical person who walked the journey to faith in Christ, and she is the figure of the church on its Spirit-filled pilgrim journey in time. She is a symbol of the communion of saints (with whom she is often pictured), and of the eschatological goal of Christian life in the mutuality and reciprocity that is the life of God. Thus one might reinterpret the exaggerated, literal, sometimes distorted, idealizing mariology of the past in a way that acknowledges the harm done to women by images of Mary's passivity. Such reinterpretations can be critical of historical excesses and theological distortions and conscious of the social and political effects of the way her symbol is used while maintaining her symbolic importance for Christian life.

The little information that is known about the historical Mary sets the limits for further symbolization. But that information allows us to say that Mary was a very human person who experienced the doubts and insecurity of historical life, the human journey in time. Somehow, in the mysterious workings of the Spirit, she came to faith in the power of Jesus' life, death, and resurrection. She, like the other disciples, received the Holy Spirit and in so doing became a part of the first Christian community, the first of the churches. Rahner notes the danger of attributing to Mary all the privileges that are in fact realizable only in the whole of humankind, especially in the church. He writes:

> Just as . . . the whole Christ is present only in head and body (of the church) together, and the body (of the church) also helps the head to reach its whole fullness, so it is analogously with Mary. It is only the church as a whole that gives reality to Mary and in its loving unity gives to this individual person her whole fullness, which she does not have when considered independently.[35]

Because Mary is the only woman specifically named in the New Testament description of Pentecost, and because the churches of east and west early described her in the christological mystery as the mother of God, she is still seen as a particular model for women. However, recent feminist discussion of the androcentric bias of human society generally and of the New Testament traditioning process in particular warns us to be cautious about the prejudices toward women implicit and explicit in the texts and in the tradition that followed. Thus her theological portrayal as one who is completely passive, obedient, and important chiefly because of her sexual characteristics is unacceptable today. Rather we must say that Mary, like the other disciples, received faith in the *active* obedience that is the *receptivity* of Christian faith.

Contemporary scholarship has demonstrated that much of the Christian tradition about women—in Augustine and Thomas Aquinas, for example—was built on an Aristotelian biology that is simply outmoded.[36] In a groundbreaking discussion more than a decade ago, Margaret Farley demonstrated that the nineteenth century discovery of the ovum as an *active* participant in the process of human conception has finally laid to rest the biological and anthropological presuppositions on which traditional theological distinctions of "masculinity" and "femininity" were based. She further pointed out that the fulfillment of individual persons and the common good are, in a Christian framework, finally ordered to the trinitarian life of God in mutuality and reciprocity, a life of dialectically fulfilled activity and receptivity. Thus the traditional distinctions of the sexes as "active" and "passive," "head" and "heart," are harmful to both individuals and the social order. Justice and Christian truth require equality, mutuality, and reciprocity in every area of human relationship. This egalitarian ethic, she suggested, has important social implications. It calls into question long-held views about the private and public domains, social roles, and the character of institutions in our society, including the church.[37]

The ramifications of Farley's views for our discussion of Mary mean that we can no longer envision her as a purely passive human figure. Rather, her receptivity to grace must be seen as fully active. Indeed, some recent discussions of Mary, including that of *Redemptoris Mater,* have stressed the importance of Mary's "fiat" in the scheme of redemption (13, 14, 39). But when we emphasize Mary's acceptance in the annunciation scene of Luke's gospel, it is important to realize that this story is theological reflection backward on an imagined scene. The historical reference, as biblical scholarship suggests, is to Mary's active receptivity to grace in the course of her whole life, in what Pope John Paul II calls her "journey of faith." The deeper symbolic meaning coalesces her life in a way that reads the past, present, and future into one moment, a moment that has been importantly provocative for the Christian imagination across the centuries.

The historical and theological excesses attendant on devotion to Mary caused real errors which attached to her figure. When reformation critics objected to the place of Marian festivals in the late medieval church, their insight was that Mary was displacing the importance of God and of Christ in authentic eucharistic or sacramental worship. As polemics increased,

Marian devotion became a kind of litmus test for Catholics who, in distinguishing themselves from Protestants, then went to further extremes in arguing for her special "privileges." Post-Trent Catholic theology went so far as to develop arguments from "fittingness," holding that it was impossible to say too much about Mary. In her regard, if God could have done it, God should have done it, and therefore God did it![38] Such excesses lent truth to the Protestant charge that Catholics divinized Mary in a kind of idolatry. Thus almost everything connected with her was excised from the Protestant Christian imagination, although there are some suggestions today about the renovation of a simple and astringent understanding of Mary in Protestant theology.[39]

The decision of the Second Vatican Council to include Mary in the *Constitution on the Church, Lumen Gentium,* righted a balance that had been askew for generations. It also placed Mary in a position that recognized her human character as related to Christ in an ecclesial context. Rather than emphasizing her special privileges, as some of the council members urged, the final text shows her as the mother of many saints, the first saint in the communion of saints.[40] She is the first disciple in the group of disciples that is the church and a human intermediary whose image suggests the solidarity of all Christians in the life of the Spirit as they journey through life in time. In the dogmas of the immaculate conception and the assumption she symbolizes both the prevenience and power of God's grace in human lives and the final transformation of human life in the fullness of God.[41]

Finally, we turn to the social and political effects of the tradition of devotion to Mary. It can be argued that no symbol is oppressive in itself but becomes so by its negative uses and effect on the lives of people.[42] Vatican Council II sought to integrate Mary into the wider framework of theological understanding in her relation to Christ and to the church, and devotion to her into the framework of eucharistic and sacramental liturgy. Today's task is the integration of faith in her, as a model of Christian faith, into the wider framework of the church's social teaching. From Leo XIII and *Rerum Novarum* to John

Paul II's controversial *Sollicitudo Rei Socialis* which appeared in 1988, the framework of Catholic social teaching cannot be separated from the uses and effects of the symbol of Mary. This connection finds its earliest theological source in Luke's gospel (1:46–55) where Mary utters the Magnificat, a song which proclaims that God has put down the mighty and exalted the humble. This biblical song of praise claims that God fills the poor with good things while sending the rich away empty. The public recitation of the Magnificat is forbidden in some Latin American countries because of its liberationist and provocative character, suggesting the close relation between our understanding of Mary and Christian social teaching (*RM* 35–37).

That teaching is committed to the rights and welfare of the poor, including laboring people in their rights of unionization, the unemployed, the homeless, and the masses of the poor in the third world. The phrase "the preferential option for the poor" epitomizes this teaching, referring to God's preference and therefore to a Christian criterion for action (*RM* 37). The most recent addition to the social teaching of the church is astute in its analysis of the dichotomy between the affluence of the northern nations and the massive poverty of the southern ones and in its criticism of both the east and the west. While human rights and initiative are curtailed in totalitarian contexts, capitalist economies tend toward materialism, consumerism and affluence for the few. The east-west blocs divert massive sums of money that might be better spent on people in order to build arms stockpiles which threaten the very life of the planet and the children of the future.[43]

Reported apparitions of Mary, often associated with the very poor or with children, are to be respected insofar as they inspire people to deeper faith and consistent action in the social arena. The pilgrimage sites of the apparitions have created what the recent papal letter calls a "geography of faith" (*RM* 28). They are to be judged by their fruits—fruits of justice, love, and peace, the criteria of the commonwealth of God that Jesus preached. As long as it is clear that they confirm and enhance the revelation which has been committed to the church in the Bible and the tradition stemming from it, these forms of popu-

lar devotion demonstrate that Christianity is not the monopoly
of scholars, exegetes, theologians, or institutional authorities.
And, as in the devotion to Our Lady of Guadalupe, they demonstrate the power of the symbol of Mary as she assimilates an
ancient religious figure into her Mexican representation and is
associated with the social and political liberation of the poor.[44]

It may be that the manifold representations of Mary across
nearly two centuries and in a variety of geographical contexts in
fact tell us more about the church in a particular situation than
about Mary. Just as the nineteenth century attributed privilege
and perfection to Mary, its ecclesiology described the church as
a perfect society. This language of perfection and idealization,
suitable only to God, led to an unbiblical, surely un-gospel-like
triumphalism and elitism on the part of the church, its authorities, its clergy, and even at times its members. In contrast, to
think of Mary today as a model of faith in the pilgrim church is
to think of her as a model for all Christians, women and men, in
the journey of faith. This understanding of Mary as a model of
the Christian on the path from unbelief to belief, a model of the
slow and often painful growth of faith as it discerns responsible
action in the tangled web of human life in time, can truly represent the pilgrim church today. A new, fully human understanding of Mary as the one who receives and communicates the
grace of Christ in the Spirit corresponds with the description of
the church as pilgrim, and all of us as persons in a community
that is on the way.

We can appreciate the images of the past tradition about
Mary, reading in them the history of Christ's church and of
human perceptions of the life of the Spirit in the church. And
we can add to that tradition the understanding of Mary today as
fully human, growing in faith, receptive to the Spirit of Christ, a
saint in the communion of saints. She reminds us, in the words
of a recent Protestant commentator, that saintliness is possible,
that we receive faith to become active Christians, that "we are
all Mary." She reminds us, he says, "that we are, in our virgin
beginnings, the humble, barefooted recipients of a grace and a
call that are the foundation of all we can ever hope to accomplish . . . she who was the simple and pure recipient of the

grace of the Holy Spirit."[45] In her biblical portrayals—the annunciation, the visitation to Elizabeth, the Christmas story, the finding of Jesus in the temple, the hidden life of Jesus with Mary at Nazareth, and the vivid scenes of Cana and Calvary—Mary is that mysterious figure of autonomy and relationship, virgin and mother, that truly reflects "the Mary in us all."

Notes

1. *Redemptoris Mater* (*RM*), March 25, 1987, *Origins* 16:43 (April 9, 1987), 745–766.
2. *Partners in the Mystery of Redemption: A Pastoral Response to Women's Concerns for Church and Society.* First Draft (*PMR*). Washington, DC: United States Catholic Conference (March 23, 1988).
3. See, e.g., Mary Daly, *Beyond God the Father: Toward a Philosophy of Women's Liberation* (Boston: Beacon, 1973), 81–82; Marina Warner, *Alone of All Her Sex: The Myth and Cult of the Virgin Mary* (New York: Wallaby, 1976), *passim.* Cf. Elizabeth A. Johnson, "The Marian Tradition and the Reality of Women," *Horizons* 12:1 (Spring 1985), 116–135.
4. Daly, 82–90.
5. Warner, 338–339.
6. Mary Gordon, "Coming to Terms with Mary," *Commonweal* CIX (January 25, 1982), 12.
7. Gottfried Marou, "Mary in Protestant Theology," tr. David Cairns, *Mary in the Churches* (Concilium 168), ed. Hans Küng and Jürgen Moltmann (New York: Seabury, 1983), 40–47. See also Theodore J. Weedon, Sr., "Mary: A Protestant Perspective," *Chicago Studies* 27:1 (April 1988), 80–95.
8. See *Mary in the New Testament,* eds. Raymond E. Brown, Karl P. Donfried, Joseph A. Fitzmyer, John Reumann (Philadelphia: Fortress, 1978).
9. See, e.g., Carol Frances Jegen, "Mary: Woman for Our World," *Chicago Studies* 27:1 (April 1988), 58.
10. Barbara Corrado Pope, "Immaculate and Powerful: The Marian Revival in the Nineteenth Century," *Immaculate*

and *Powerful: The Female in Sacred Image and Social Reality*, ed. Clarissa W. Atkinson, Constance H. Buchanan and Margaret R. Miles. The Harvard Women's Studies in Religion Series (Boston: Beacon, 1985), 173–200.

11. *Ibid.*, 195.
12. Lawrence Cunningham, *Mother of God* (San Francisco: Harper & Row, 1982), 121.
13. See Warner, *passim*.
14. Gordon, 11. See Fredrick M. Jelly, "Characteristics of Contemporary Mariology," *Chicago Studies* 27:1 (April 1988), 63–79.
15. "Motherhood or Friendship," tr. Margaret Kohl, *Mary in the Churches*, 17–22.
16. Donal Flanagan, *The Theology of Mary* (Hales Corners, WI: Clergy Book Service, 1976), 97.
17. *The Feminine Dimension of the Divine* (Philadelphia: Westminster, 1979), 122–133.
18. *Mary—The Feminine Face of the Church* (Philadelphia: Westminster, 1977).
19. "Feminist Spirituality, Christian Identity and Catholic Vision," *Womanspirit Rising*, ed. Carol P. Christ and Judith Plaskow (San Francisco: Harper & Row, 1979), 136–148.
20. *Models of God: Theology for an Ecological, Nuclear Age* (Philadelphia: Fortress, 1987), 97–187.
21. See Elizabeth A. Johnson, "The Incomprehensibility of God and the Image of God Male and Female," *Theological Studies* 45:3 (September 1984), 441–480.
22. "The Mother of Jesus in the New Testament," *Mary in the Churches*, 10.
23. *Ibid.*, 3–11.
24. *Ibid.*, 8. Cf. Patrick J. Bearsley, "Mary, the Perfect Disciple," *Theological Studies* 41:3 (September 1980), 461–504.
25. *Ibid.*, 9 (italics removed).
26. See Wolfhart Pannenberg, *Jesus—God and Man*, 2nd ed., tr. Lewis L. Wilkins and Duane A. Priebe (Philadelphia: Westminster, 1977), especially 21–37; Karl Rahner, *Theological Investigations 13*, 54. David Bourke (New York: Seabury, 1975), 189–223; Rahner, *Theological Investigations*

17, tr. Margaret Kohl (New York: Crossroad, 1981), 3–50; Edward Schillebeeckx, *Jesus: An Experiment in Christology,* tr. Hubert Hoskins (New York: Seabury, 1979); Schillebeeckx, *Christ: The Experience of Jesus as Lord,* tr. John Bowden (New York: Seabury, 1980).

27. Pannenberg, e.g., 33–36, 39–42, 153–156, 184–188; Schillebeeckx, *Interim Report on the Books Jesus and Christ,* tr. John Bowden (New York: Crossroad, 1981), 27–49, 64–104.

28. Rahner, "The Two Basic Types of Christology," *Theological Investigations 13,* 213–223.

29. Schillebeeckx, *Interim Report,* 29–35.

30. "Mary and Contemporary Christology: Rahner and Schillebeeckx," *Eglise et Theologie* 15 (1984), 155–182. Cf. Karl Rahner, *Mary, Mother of the Lord,* tr. W. J. O'Hare (New York: Herder and Herder, 1963, orig. 1956); Edward Schillebeeckx, *Mary, Mother of the Redemption,* tr. N. D. Smith (New York: Sheed and Ward, 1964, orig. 1954).

31. Richard Kugelman, "Presenting Mary to Today's Catholics," *Marian Studies* 22 (Dayton: Mariological Society of America, 1971), 50–53.

32. See Anne Carr, "Mary in the Mystery of the Church: Vatican Council II," *Mary According to Women,* ed. Carol Frances Jegen (Kansas City: Leaven, 1985), 5–32 for details and bibliography.

33. Kari Børresen, "Mary in Catholic Theology," *Mary in the Churches,* 48–56.

34. "The Symbolic Character of Theological Statements about Mary," *Journal of Ecumenical Studies* 22:2 (Spring 1985), 312–335.

35. "Mary and the Christian Image of Women," *Theological Investigations 19,* tr. Edward Quinn (New York: Crossroad, 1983), 214.

36. See Kari Børresen, *Subordination and Equivalence: The Nature and Role of Women in Augustine and Thomas Aquinas,* tr. Charles H. Talbot (Washington, DC: University Press of America, 1981).

37. Margaret Farley, "New Patterns of Relationship: Begin-

nings of a Moral Revolution," *Theological Studies* 36:4 (December 1975), 627–646; reprinted in *Woman: New Dimensions,* ed. Walter Burghardt (New York: Paulist, 1977).

38. McKenzie, 7; Cunningham, 68–71.
39. Marou, 45–46.
40. For an analysis of the formation of the texts dealing with Mary at Vatican II, see Michael O'Carroll, "Vatican II and Our Lady's Mediation," *Irish Theological Quarterly* 37 (1970), 24–55.
41. Carol Frances Jegen, "Mary Immaculate: Woman of Freedom, Patroness of the United States," *Mary According to Women,* 143–163; Carr, *ibid.,* 19–26.
42. See Anne Carr, *Transforming Grace: Christian Tradition and Women's Experience* (San Francisco: Harper & Row, 1988), 108–109.
43. See the encyclical of John Paul II, *Sollicitudo Rei Socialis, National Catholic Reporter* (Vol. 24, No. 31) May 27, 1988, 14–27.
44. See Virgil Elizondo, "Mary and the Poor: A Model of Evangelizing," *Mary in the Churches,* 59–65.
45. Ronald Gotez, "The Mary in Us All," *The Christian Century* 104:37 (December 9, 1987), 1108–1109.

Mary and the Image of God

Elizabeth Johnson

INTRODUCTION

Throughout the course of its history the Catholic religious spirit has honored in a plethora of ways the person of Mary of Nazareth, that New Testament disciple of Jesus Christ who was also his mother. Her historically irreplaceable personal involvement in the birth of the Messiah coupled with her own lifelong faith in God gave impetus to the sense that in some way she was intimately linked with the mystery of the world's salvation. Consequently she has been esteemed and praised with deep affection and petitioned for aid in spiritual and material need. The power of this connection intuited between the figure of Mary and the saving mystery which surrounds the world has led to a popular devotion of vast and diverse proportions, as well as to doctrinal pronouncements and theological reflections, some more exuberant than others.

From the time of the reformation onward, thinkers of that tradition have criticized many aspects of this phenomenon, arguing that for all practical intents and purposes the figure of Mary has slipped the bounds of mere creaturehood and either competed with the person of Jesus Christ who is the sole mediator between God and human beings (1 Tim 2:5), or at times even replaced him. Official Catholic sensitivity to this concern is apparent in the eighth chapter of Vatican II's *Constitution on the Church,* so constructed that Mary's role is seen to be not separate from the mystery of Christ and the church but rather integrated within them.[1] This doctrinal teaching emphasizes that Christ alone is mediator while Mary, an altogether singular and preeminent member of the church with a special role to play in salvation history, is yet one with the human race in need of salvation. It likewise cautions in earnest against exaggeration, emotionalism, and vain credulity in devotion to Mary. Yet, a number of thorny theological difficulties continue to be ecumenically unresolved; and while interest in the figure of Mary has declined among many post-conciliar Catholics in the western democracies, other areas of the world show continuing and even growing Marian emphasis, some of which remains open to the reformation charge of distorting the gospel.

Study of the development of this Marian tradition shows that much of its growth is not explainable simply by the exigencies of preaching the gospel: despite correct official formulations, more is going on here than immediately meets the eye. A surprisingly diverse number of scholars have proposed that one of the primary reasons for the growth and power of the Marian phenomenon throughout history lies in the symbolic force of her figure which, precisely as a female representation, bears images of God otherwise excluded from the mainline Christian perception of God as Father and Son and Spirit. In other words, images of God as female, arguably necessary for the full expression of the mystery of God but suppressed from official formulations, have migrated to the figure of this woman. Consequently, in devotion to her as a close, compassionate mother who will not let one of her children be lost, what is actually being mediated is a most appealing experience of God. Mary, it has been argued, has embodied aspects of divine reality best symbolized in female form. For innumerable believers the person of this woman has functioned to reveal divine love as merciful, close, interested, always ready to hear and respond to human needs, inspiring trust, and profoundly attractive, and has done so to a degree not possible when one thinks of God simply as a ruling male person or persons.

Most scholars who have posited this relation between the

figure of Mary and imagery of the divine have been content to let the issue rest there. However, under the pressure of the theological necessity to envision God more adequately in ways inclusive of female reality, another step may be taken. This would be the retrieval of those elements in the Marian symbol which properly belong to divine reality, and the direct attribution of them to God imaged as female. If Mary reflects the female face of God, then Marian theology and devotion have a contribution to make toward the crucial task of imaging God in inclusive fashion. In other words, the Marian tradition is a golden motherlode which can be "mined" in order to retrieve female imagery and language about the holy mystery of God.[2] This is admittedly an open issue. The purpose of this theological study is to test this hypothesis, judging its viability by the results it produces.[3]

As a first step we will conduct a reconnaissance of the positions of key scholars who have explicitly argued that the figure of Mary has in fact borne imagery of the divine in the Christian tradition. Ten representative approaches to the issue are examined, all drawn from differing fields of scholarship or, in the case of theological interpretations, from differing schools of thought. While all of the thinkers considered do posit the connection between Mary and female imagery of the divine, they envision and explain the relationship differently. In the process of exploring these diverse angles of vision, we will be looking for hermeneutical clues which may shed light on precisely how the Marian tradition may serve the task of re-imagining God in female symbols.

On the basis of the intrinsic relation between the figure of Mary and divine imagery uncovered in the initial survey, the second part of this study will suggest certain elements in the Marian tradition which can be transferred to a fully inclusive idea of God. In the process of this exploration, doctrinal, ecumenical, and feminist interests converge. Restoring to the holy mystery those elements borne by the figure of Mary can be one contribution toward a doctrine of God freed from the biases and restrictions of patriarchy. Concomitantly, relieving the figure of Mary of its historic burden of imaging God in female form can also remove from the Marian tradition one source of its tendency to distortion and set it more firmly on a gospel path, to ecumenical advantage. Both of these moves—imaging God as a female acting subject and retrieving Mary as a genuine woman whose life was a journey of faith—can serve the insight that all women have an unsurpassable dignity as human beings made in the image of God, a truth which is struggling at this moment of *kairos* to come to expression in theory and practice. The triple wager I am making as we begin is that the Marian tradition has a great deal to offer to a more adequate theology of God, that once this offer is received the Marian tradition itself will be fundamentally redirected and refreshed, and that consequently one obstacle to the church becoming a community of equal disciples will be diminished.

PRESUPPOSITIONS

Several basic premises guide the investigation undertaken here. First, given the present state of scholarship, I take it as a well-established thesis that the holy mystery has been and can be referred to in ways reflective of the reality of women. Not only did the biblical and later Christian traditions occasionally use this kind of language, thus providing a basis for its legitimacy, but theologically it can be argued that such references are necessary if the truths of the incomprehensibility of the divine mystery and the human dignity and equality of women are to emerge.[4] The holy mystery of God transcends all images and concepts, but God's created world, the world of nature and the human world of women and men, can separately or together serve as metaphor, analogy, or symbol pointing to, naming, and evoking the mystery. This investigation, then, is set within the parameters of the contemporary discussion about proper symbolizing of God.

Second, I find truth in the thesis that the Christian tradition's patriarchy with its accompanying androcentric structures of thought has shortchanged the fullness of religious language and imagery of the divine, locking the divine mystery into the single predominant image of a male person or persons. This distortion is reflected in mirror fashion in the Marian tradition, where what was going homeless in official doctrine found a home and flourished. One of the strongest insights into the compensatory nature of the Marian tradition was articulated by Teilhard de Chardin, who was convinced that the cult of Mary served to satisfy an "irresistible Christian need" in the church, namely, the need to correct "a dreadfully masculinized" conception of the Godhead.[5] When the dogma of Mary's assumption into heaven was defined, he wrote that he was "too conscious of the bio-psychological necessity of the 'Marian'—to counterbalance the 'masculinity' of Yahweh—not to feel the profound need for this gesture." The difference between Teilhard's insight and the guiding idea here lies in the fact that this state of affairs is now recognized to be the result of patriarchy and subject to reform, rather than necessarily definitive and in need of compensation.

Third, it seems evident to me that what has been displaced from religious imagery and language about God rightfully belongs back with God. Once it is not so unthinkable to envision the holy mystery in gender-inclusive ways, then the Marian tradition can yield its powerful maternal and other female images of the divine, which can be directly attributed to God. Primordially, God is our loving mother who will not let one of her children be lost; God the Mother is the ever compassionate one to whom we entrust our needs; etc. The figure of Mary no longer has to bear the burden of keeping alive female imagery of the divine once the holy mystery is more fully envisioned.

Fourth, while psychology, cultural anthropology and social history have analyzed the Marian tradition from the perspectives of their own operating principles, the exploration here is primarily theological. Thus, the criteria for discerning where the image of God may be being borne by another symbol are derived from the scriptures, from the classical doctrine of God, and from liturgical praise of God. Initially stated, wherever in the tradition Mary is described or addressed in such a way that the ultimacy of the holy mystery as reflected in scripture, doctrine or liturgy is evoked, and wherever the ultimacy of the believer's trust is correspondingly elicited, there it can be sup-

posed that the reality of God is being named in female metaphors.

Finally, I take issue with the idea that Mary represents the
feminine dimension of the divine, and gives us an insight into
that "side" of God's reality. Those who hold such a position
almost inevitably make use of some interpretation of Jungian
theory with its accompanying labeling of certain human characteristics as masculine or feminine. As this works out in theology, the predominant image of God remains that of the male,
but one tempered by the nurturing and maternal traits reflected in Mary. The female of itself is not allowed to function
as an icon of the divine in all fullness. By contrast, I would
argue that Mary no more reveals the feminine dimension of
God than Jesus reveals the masculine dimension of God. In my
judgment, God does not have a feminine dimension; nor a
masculine dimension; nor an animal dimension (to be arrived at
from the image of God as a great mother bird protecting her
little ones under her wings); nor a mineral dimension (from the
image of God the rock); etc. Images and names of God do not
aim at part of the divine mystery, were that even possible, but
intend to evoke the whole. Consequently, female imagery by
itself points to God as such, and has the capacity to represent
God not only as nurturing, although certainly that, but as powerful, initiating, creating-redeeming-saving, and victorious over
the powers of this world. If women are created in the image of
God, then God can be imaged in female metaphors in as full
and as limited a way as God is imaged in male ones, without talk
of feminine dimensions or sides or traits reducing the impact of
this imagery.

As an initial step, then, in retrieving images of the divine
from the Marian tradition, we first establish the very existence
of the Mary-God connection through a select survey of scholarly thought in the fields of history of religions, history of doctrine, systematic theology, feminist and liberation theology,
psychology of religion, social science, and ecumenical thought.
The consensus emerging from all of these fields indicates that
there is indeed an intrinsic relation between the figure of

Mary that has developed in the Christian tradition and the idea of God.

INTERPRETATIONS OF MARY AND THE FEMALE FACE OF GOD

1. Scholars of early Christian history who have studied the origin of the links between the figure of Mary and imagery of the divine have found morphological similarities between the post-Constantinian ecclesial cult of Mary and the pervasive cults of the great mother in the Mediterranean world into which Christianity was moving. Very little is known precisely about how elements of the Hellenistic cults of female deities accrued to the person of Mary but, as Hugo Rahner notes in the course of his argument for the essential differences between them, such similarities at least in superficially observable matters are simply a matter of historical fact.[6] The church was not fashioned in a vacuum but absorbed many of the assumptions, verbal and visual imagery, and rituals of the surrounding culture into its own theology and liturgy, in a process which affected not only the presentation of Mary but also of Jesus Christ, the martyrs and saints, and even the holy mystery of God.

In his classic study of this adaptation in the case of Mary, Jean Daniélou begins by stressing the radical distinction between the mystery cults and the Christian veneration of Mary.[7] Insofar as the latter originated in an historically unique revelation of God in Jesus Christ, and furthermore portrayed Mary as virginal rather than as sexually fecund earth mother, there is more dissimilarity than similarity between them. Once these essential differences are established, Daniélou argues, one is then free to examine the ways in which Christianity's Marian cult adapted elements from the mystery cults and substituted itself—historically in the fourth century world, and psychologically in the human spirit—for the cults wherein the female deities played an absolutely central role. The officials of the church allowed this assimilation of pagan elements for two reasons: it was an excellent missionary strategy in a world where

female deities were so highly honored, and it reflected a sacramental view of reality in which, once "baptized" and purified of
its ancient content, any symbol could evoke the God revealed in
Christ. Among the people, however, it must be asked whether
such purification was actually accomplished, or whether instead
in a form of syncretism the cult of Mary simply continued the
veneration of the maternal power of the female deities. In either case, Daniélou concludes, the power of the Marian cult,
founded on a free decision by God, lies in the fact that it
corresponds to the aspirations of the human heart, having psychologically parallel functions to the cult of the great mother
goddesses.

Other students of historical development have identified
innumerable concrete ways in which this adaptation was accomplished. Places in nature where female deities had been
honored with pilgrimage and prayer became associated with
Mary: grottoes, springs, promontories, mountains, lakes,
woods.[8] Shrines and temples to the goddess were rededicated
to Mary the mother of God, outstanding examples being found
in Rome, Athens, Chartres, and Ephesus (it being generally
conceded to be no accident that the doctrine of the *Theotokos*
was proclaimed to an enthusiastic population in the same city
where in the time of Paul the people had demonstrated in favor
of their great goddess Diana—Acts 19:23–41). Artistic symbols
of the goddess accrued to Mary: her dark blue cloak, turreted
crown, link with the moon and the stars, with water and wind.
The iconography of Mary seated with her child facing outward
on her lap was arguably patterned on the pose of Isis with
Horus, the mother herself an upright royal throne on which the
god-king was presented to the world.[9] In hymns reminiscent of
the aretalogies of Isis she was praised with titles and attributes
of female deities, as all-holy, merciful, wise, the universal
mother, giver of fertility and the blessings of life, protector of
pregnant women and their children, sailors at sea, and all who
called to her in need; in prayers patterned on petitions to the
great mother, Mary was directly invoked as protector and asked
to deliver simple people from danger.[10] The still-venerated
statues of the black madonna at Le Puy, Montserrat, Chartres,

etc. derive from ancient black stones connected with the fertility power of maternal deities, black being the beneficent color of subterranean and uterine fecundity. Adapted into the iconography of the classic Gallo-Roman mother goddesses, this symbolism was then conserved in the sculpted images of the black virgin.[11] One of the most striking examples of popular adaptation of indigenous symbolism took place in central Sicily where a church to Mary was built over a temple dedicated to Ceres/Demeter and her daughter Persephone. Until Pius IX ordered it removed, an ancient statue of the goddess and her child had been used to represent Mary and the infant Jesus, despite the fact that the sculpted child was female.[12] In at least one instance popular assimilation of the goddess cult to Mary destroyed the fundamental structure of Christian faith. The fourth century sect of the Collyridians, made up mostly of women, worshiped Mary as divine, offering sweet cakes before her throne as had so many before them to the great mother. Against them Epiphanius, bishop of Salamis (d. 403), inveighed, "The body of Mary is holy but she is not God. . . . Let no one adore Mary."[13]

For all the real differences in structure and content between Christian faith and the mystery cults, the evidence at hand indicates a strong process of assimilation and adaptation of ideas and verbal and artistic imagery in the case of the emerging cult of Mary. As Daniélou argues, while remaining independent, Christianity yet used the rich symbols of paganism purified of their ancient content to express its own revelation, and thereby insinuated itself into the hearts of new believers so recently accustomed to the beneficence and maternal power of the female deities. This comparative approach to the origin of Marian symbolism yields an interpretive principle for the present study: the Marian tradition is one conduit of imagery and language about divine reality flowing from the veneration of the great mother in the pre-Christian Mediterranean world. Even when well-integrated into a Christian gestalt, the historical origin of this symbolism opens up the possibility of drawing upon it to reflect upon the holy mystery in female metaphors.

2. Scholars of the medieval European period, document-
ing its extensive growth in popular devotion and learned speculation about Mary, inevitably note that by the sixteenth century
her figure had taken on divinized attributes and functions bor-
rowed not from the ancient goddess but from the Christian
Trinity itself.[14] While the Protestant reformers roundly criticized this development and while the Catholic reform sought to
correct it, more contemporary interpreters have perceived it as
a quest for religious experience through the feminine image
and what it connotes, an experience not available through the
idea of God of the time.[15]

The dynamic of the medieval Marian phenomenon is complex. Theologically, the scholastic systematization of Hellenistic
thought patterns lifted up the supposition that the female/ma-
ternal was and perforce had to be totally absent from God, for
it was intrinsic to the maternal to be passive, in potency, and
receptive. Since God is pure act, only the active power of the
masculine/paternal could be allowed to enter the notion of
"him."[16] The scholarly medieval idea of God consequently became ever more rigorously androcentric.

On a popular level, the growth of medieval devotion to
Mary is most frequently attributed to theology's emphasis on
the transcendent justice of God, which made it impossible for
God to forgive sin without demanding satisfaction (cf. Anselm),
and on a correlative image of Christ as righteous judge. Sinful
people felt existentially that their salvation was a precarious
thing, with the temptations of Satan ever-present and the
danger of eternal torment in hell very real. In this scenario, the
divine saving quality of mercy found its expression in the wom-
anly figure of Mary, who could be trusted as a mother to understand people's sinful inadequacies, and relied upon as
queen to plead their case before her son. Added to this was the
simple fact of a hard and dangerous life lived by masses of
people who found in their mother someone who would be
interested and help, not only with the blessing of salvation but
with everyday, earthly blessings as well.[17] Consequently, enormous veneration was poured out toward Mary, expressed in the

multiplication of feasts, prayers, relics, titles, works of art, shrines, cathedrals, pilgrimages, and narrations of miracles.

In the process, Mary at first paralleled and then occasionally outshone God the Father and especially God the Son. The power and creativity of God the Father was mirrored in Mary who by virtue of her role at the incarnation which gave the world the Savior was in some way creative of all that was renewed. As Anselm wrote, "So God is the Father of all created things, and Mary is the Mother of all recreated things."[18] Veneration directed to her in light of her recreative power included such acts as rewriting the psalms in order to substitute Mary for God as the acting subject of divine deeds and consequently as recipient of praise:

> Sing to Our Lady a new song, for she hath done wonderful things. In the sight of the nations she hath revealed her mercy; her name is heard even to the ends of the earth.[19]

Similarly, standard hymns of divine praise such as the Te Deum were refashioned to honor Mary:

> We praise thee, O Mother of God; we confess thee, Mary ever Virgin. . . . Thee all angels and archangels, thrones and principalities serve. Thee all powers and virtues of heaven and all dominations obey. Before thee all the angelic choirs, the cherubim and seraphim, exulting, stand. With unceasing voice every angelic creature proclaims thee: Holy, holy, holy, Mary Virgin Mother of God![20]

In time, Mary was gifted with omniscience and a certain omnipotence over heaven, earth and hell. Biblical affirmations of God the Father were attributed to her: e.g. she so loved the world that she gave her only son (Jn 3:16).[21] She could be prayed to as Our Mother who art in heaven, and asked to give us each day our daily bread. In moments of critical reflection there was universal insistence that these and similar honors redounded to the glory of God who "himself" had so honored Mary. In effect, however, this kind of devotion to the mother of God was actually devotion to God the Mother, to the ultimate mystery of the creative and recreative God glimpsed in female form.

It was especially in the area of Jesus Christ's redemptive activity that Mary's parallelism with divine reality grew strong. While Jesus Christ was acknowledged as gracious Savior, his function of judging frequently overshadowed the quality of his mercy, which in turn was attributed abundantly to Mary. Innumerable writers followed the line of thinking reflected in an influential thirteenth century sermon, attributed to Bonaventure, which proclaimed that the kingdom of God was divided into two zones, justice and mercy; Mary had the better part because she was made queen of mercy, while her son was king of justice, and "mercy is better than justice."[22] She was then depicted as restraining Christ's wrath, placing back into its sheath his sword which was raging against sinful humanity. As the period progressed, she went from being merciful mediatrix with the just judge to being sharer of common dominion with Christ through the pain she suffered on Calvary, and thence to power over the mercy of Christ whom she commanded by her maternal authority. So great was the essential role of Mary's mercy that medieval theologians wrote of her what biblical authors wrote of Christ: in her the fullness of the Godhead dwelt corporeally (Col 2:9); of her fullness we have all received (Jn 1:16); because she had emptied herself God had highly exalted her, so that at her name every knee should bow (Phil 2:5–11). As even a brief sampling makes clear, the medieval parallels between Mary and Christ in nature, grace and glory, in virtue and dignity, resulted in the figure of Mary assuming divine prerogatives. As co-redemptrix, she merited salvation; as mediatrix, she obtained grace for sinners; as queen and mother of mercy, she dispensed it herself. All of this power resided in Mary as a maternal woman, who could be trusted to understand and cope with human weakness better than could a somewhat testy God the Father or a just Jesus Christ. In her person she represented ultimate graciousness over against divine severity.

Hence she was the recipient of sinners' basic trust and affection.

Without in any way condoning the abuses to which such a development led, the perspective of our inquiry opens the way to see that late medieval mariology demonstrates the capacity of female imagery to model the redemptive activity of God. The medieval transfer to Mary of Christ's attribute of mercy resulted in the figure of Mary functioning as a female image of the christological mystery. Her powerful role as mediatrix offered a female icon of Christ's intercessory role. Her unfailing compassion and will to save modeled the soteriological good news in the figure of a woman. The theological distortions of the period were very real, yet the phenomenon offers another interpretive principle for our inquiry: especially where the Marian tradition breaks the boundaries of the structure of biblical and traditional faith, there one can look for a source of female metaphors for the ultimate saving mystery of the divine, created by a dynamic of compensation for an over-masculinized and harsh, i.e. deficient patriarchal concept of God.

3. As the Roman Catholic tradition developed after the reformation, systematic theology made clear the priority of God and the centrality of Christ in the mystery of salvation. There was still room, however, to attribute to Mary an important function in the revelation of God's love. In a highly influential work written a decade before the Second Vatican Council, Edward Schillebeeckx reasoned that while God's love is both paternal and maternal, the latter quality is not and cannot be explicated in the man Jesus because of his maleness.[23] Thus God chose Mary, so that this maternal aspect of divine love might be represented in her person. All that is tender, mild, simple, generous, gentle, and sweet in God is manifest in her. As a partner to Christ, she explicates in her figure as a woman God's maternal redeeming love: "Mary is the translation and effective expression in maternal terms of God's mercy, grace and redeeming love which manifested itself to us in a visible and tangible form in the person of Christ, our Redeemer."[24] What is so interesting in this treatment of the theme is the choice of active verbs to express a relationship:

Mary represents, makes manifest, explicates, translates, effectively expresses something of God which cannot come to light in Jesus Christ, redeemer though he be. This quality is the feminine and maternal aspect of divine love, which needs expression through the figure of a woman. Schillebeeckx's interpretation thus identifies the revelatory capacity of the figure of this woman not only in a situation of distortion and abuse, as at the end of the middle ages, but even within the context of a rightly ordered reflection on faith. God's love, revealed paradigmatically in the person of Christ, needs a further translation into feminine terms to be fully expressed. Thus, in still another thought system, the path between Marian imagery and the fuller expression of divine mystery is laid.

Schillebeeckx's statement is one of the most explicit theological treatments of the thesis we are pursuing. While it is doubtful that he would treat the subject in the same way today, having repudiated the major categories of objective and subjective redemption within which he worked out his pre-conciliar mariology,[25] nevertheless it stands as a testimony to the need for something more than is expressed in a patriarchal view of the revelation of God in Christ, and to the fulfilling of that need in the person of Mary. Schillebeeckx's reduction of the feminine to the maternal, and of the maternal to mildness and sweetness, is highly questionable in light of the experience of real women and of feminist reflection today. Nevertheless, he was searching for an envisionment of God's saving reality in all its fullness. His thesis, shaped in the context of counter-reformation mariology, provides a hermeneutic of that mariology's dynamism; namely it expressed aspects of divine saving reality in the figure of Mary.

4. In the ecumenical climate since the Second Vatican Council, a more precise analysis of the function of Mary in expressing divine reality has become a focus of attention. Catholic theologians such as Yves Congar, René Laurentin, L.J. Cardinal Suenens, and Heribert Mühlen have paid careful attention to the Protestant critique that in the Catholic tradition the action and experience of Mary have substituted in a particular way for the action and experience of God the Holy Spirit.[26]

Catholics have said of Mary that she forms Christ in them, that she is spiritually present to guide and inspire, that she is the link between themselves and Christ, and that one goes to Jesus through her. But are these not precisely the roles of the Spirit of Christ? Furthermore, Mary is called intercessor, mediatrix, helper, advocate, defender, consoler, counselor. But are these not titles which belong more primordially to the Paraclete (see Jn 14:16 and 26; 15:26; 16:7)? Catholics have thought and preached as Leo XIII did, saying that "Every grace granted to man has three degrees in order; for by God it is communicated to Christ, from Christ it passes to the Virgin, and from the Virgin it descends to us."[27] Is this not a dislocation of the Holy Spirit, who is essential to the trinitarian gift of grace in this world? The observation of Protestant student Elsie Gibson has been frequently quoted as Catholic thinkers have attempted to come to grips with this issue:

> When I began the study of Catholic theology, every place I expected to find an exposition of the doctrine of the Holy Spirit, I found Mary. What Protestants universally attribute to the action of the Holy Spirit was attributed to Mary.[28]

Finding this critique basically substantiated, Laurentin has observed that this Marian development occupied spaces left vacant by an undeveloped pneumatology in medieval Latin theology and even more in post-tridentine theology. The way forward, he suggests, is to be found by a return to the scriptures. There the Spirit has obvious primacy while Mary is overshadowed by, filled with, made fruitful by, and enabled to prophesy in the power of the Spirit. Consequently, the privileged sign and witness of the Holy Spirit in the community of the church is the person of Mary, whose role of mediation and intercession occurs only within the primordial role of the Spirit.

More light is shed on this angle by patristic studies which have shown how the Holy Spirit was pictured as Mother in certain forms of early Syriac Christianity. The Spirit's image was that of the brooding or hovering mother bird, mothering Jesus

into life at his conception and into mission at his baptism, and
bringing believers to birth and mission in the waters of baptism.
This doctrine of the motherhood of the Spirit fostered a spirituality of warmth which found expression in characteristic
prayers:

> As the wings of doves over their nestlings,
> And the mouths of their nestlings toward their mouths,
> So also are the wings of the Spirit over my heart.[29]

This motherhood imagery eventually accrued to the church
(holy mother the church) and to Mary, once again occasioning
the situation where the figure of this woman became the bearer
of profoundly important characteristics of God. The action of
the Holy Spirit, who is the most anthropomorphically amor-
phous of the persons of the Trinity and also the most function-
ally connected with divine intimacy and presence to human
beings has been concretized in the imputed actions of the figure of Mary. This suggests another hermeneutic for dealing
with the Marian tradition: we may test for how many elements
of a proper theology of the Spirit of God are embedded in the
affirmations made about this woman, and retrieve those elements for use in reconstructing an inclusive idea of God.

To summarize our explorations to this point: soundings of
the Marian tradition's historical origin, medieval over-develop-
ment, and post-reformation systematization reveal workable
connections between the figure of Mary and the idea of God in
both popular piety and theological reflection (and there is not a
hard and fast distinction between these two). Roughly corre-
sponding to each of these three periods, the figure of Mary has
taken on characteristics of the creating, saving and sanctifying
God, functioning to some degree in a compensatory way vis-à-
vis the three divine persons of Father, Son, and Spirit.

5. Interpreters of Latin American Catholicism universally
note that massive devotion to Mary is one of the most popular,
persistent, and original characteristics of its people's piety.
From one contemporary perspective, that of liberation theology, the enduring devotion of powerless, defeated, and poor

people to the dark-skinned, sorrowing madonna who also sings of liberation (the "Magnificat," Lk 1:46–55) signals Mary's identification with the oppressed in the name of God. Consequently, her cult expressly validates the dignity of each downtrodden person and galvanizes energy for resistance against dominating powers.[30]

Pastoral theologian Virgil Elizondo, however, argues further that from the perspective of the development of doctrine this phenomenon points not only to the liberation of downtrodden peoples but also to the liberation of a restrictive idea of God. The origin of devotion to Our Lady of Guadalupe, for example, involved resistance by conquered people not only to the European invaders, but to the male God in whose name they dominated. In the process of this resistance, the people became the recipients of a major disclosure in the development of the Christian understanding of God. Similar to studies of the origin of the Marian cult in the fourth century, analysis of the genesis of this Mexican cult supports this contention.[31] The place of the original apparition was the site of an ancient temple dedicated to Tonantzin, the Indian virgin mother of the gods. The flowers and music of the vision were part of Tonantzin's temple worship. The dark skin of the woman of the apparition, the language she spoke, the colors she was wearing and the celestial symbols surrounding her were all reminiscent of the goddess of the defeated people. Yet it was not Tonantzin who was appearing, but the virgin mother of the Christian God. As Elizondo interprets the creative result of this cross-cultural encounter, the figure of Our Lady of Guadalupe set within the complex of Christian doctrine combined the Indian female expression of God, which the Spanish had tried to wipe out as diabolical, with the Spanish male expression of God which the Indians had found incomprehensible (for everything which is perfect in the Nahuatl cosmovision has a male and female component). Each understanding of God was expanded by the other, yielding a new mestizo expression which enriches the very understanding of the selfhood of God. In order to appreciate this, one must proceed through the ways of thought of the oppressed poor of the new world. If one is willing to make the journey, the full theological implication of Marian devotion for disclosure of the mystery of God will begin to emerge. In Elizondo's evocative phrase, "The Marian devotion of the poor leads the universal Church to a new appreciation of the very selfhood of God."[32] What such devotion carries is the experience of the ultimate reality of God through female imagery.

Thus, the cult of Our Lady of Guadalupe is not simply a conduit for female imagery of God belonging to an ancient religion now disappeared. Rather, in its present effectiveness as a vehicle of religious experience this cult mediates the compassionate reality of God in the form of a woman. The figure of Guadalupe is a living locus of female imagery of the divine.

6. An even stronger case is made by Latin American theologian Leonardo Boff, who carries explicit reflection on Mary's relation to deity a giant step further than has until now occurred. This he does with the idea, put forward as a hypothesis, that just as the human nature of Jesus is assumed by the Logos, so too Mary should be considered as hypostatically united to the third person of the Holy Trinity:

> We maintain the hypothesis that the Virgin Mary, Mother of God and of all men and women, realizes the feminine absolutely and eschatologically, inasmuch as the Holy Spirit has made her his temple, sanctuary, and tabernacle in so real and genuine a way that she is to be regarded as hypostatically united to the Third Person of the Blessed Trinity.[33]

There is an essential difference between the incarnation of the Logos in Jesus and the union of the Holy Spirit with Mary; but the latter union is an ontological one so profound that the Spirit can be said to have taken flesh in the Virgin Mary, who in turn personifies the Spirit.

Two major presuppositions underlie Boff's hypothesis: one, the venerable Catholic understanding that human nature as such is created with a capacity for the hypostatic union; the other, the more controverted idea that the Holy Spirit is the divine person by whom the feminine is appropriated. While in

the incarnation Jesus Christ assumed human nature in its total-
ity, still it is the masculine which is assumed in direct and immediate fashion, while the feminine is assumed and divinized only
indirectly as a secondary component of the male. Conscious of
the long-standing subordination of women, Boff argues that it
is only fitting that the feminine itself should also be assumed
and sanctified directly and immediately. This occurs in Mary,
immaculately conceived, virgin mother of God, assumed into
heaven, and co-redemptrix and co-mediatrix of salvation. In
her, the feminine is "hypostatically assumed" by the Spirit, with
the result that the created feminine is now eternally associated
with the mystery of the being of God and is a vehicle of God's
own self-realization. Mary rightly belongs not under Christ but
by his side; widespread attribution to her of the functions of the
Holy Spirit is legitimate.

While obviously reflecting the *lex orandi* of millions of people in the Latin American church, Boff's hypothesis has come
in for severe criticism.[34] The point to note for our purpose is
that, unlike theologians who would judge maximalist tendencies
in the cult of Mary to be compensatory for a distorted, over-
masculinized image of God, Boff is seeking to legitimize this
development by proposing that Mary as a woman is ontologically divinized to the point of being the human embodiment of
the Holy Spirit. As such, her figure as a woman is rightly revelatory of divine characteristics usually associated with the Spirit
of God, such as all-encompassing warmth and love, immediate
presence, inspiring energy, intimacy, and care for the weak and
little ones.

7. Feminist theologians have consistently argued for the
legitimacy of imaging the incomprehensible holy mystery in
terms taken from the reality and experience of women as well as
men, finding long-neglected examples of this kind of naming in
the biblical and theological traditions. In this context, the Marian tradition has come in for its own scrutiny. Remembering
her own childhood in Catholic Bavaria, for example, Elisabeth
Schüssler Fiorenza has analyzed from an experiential point of
view what Schillebeeckx was stating in more theoretical form.[35]
In that time and place, the God presented for belief had been

shaped by a long process of patriarchalization as a result of which the divine image became ever more remote and judgmental. Mary became the beloved "other face" of God, the figure who bore the life-giving, compassionate, caring, saving, and closely intimate qualities so characteristic of the Abba whom Jesus preached. On the intellectual level a distinction was maintained between adoration of God and veneration of Mary, but on the affective, imaginative level, the Catholic child experienced the love of God and the saving mystery of divine reality in the figure of this woman. Schüssler Fiorenza's analysis leads her to conclude that the Catholic cult of Mary is one fruitful source of theological discourse which speaks of the divine in female terms, images and symbols.

Two insights here prove useful for the analysis of relation between the figure of Mary and the image of God. The development of a compassion-oriented mariology is directly related to an over-emphasis on a masculinized image of God, and functions as a remedy for what is lacking in such an image. Furthermore, the qualities attributed to Mary in such a development properly belong to the holy mystery. They should be transferred back to that source, so that the reality of the divine is thought ontologically to be compassionate, intimate, and caring, and is imaged to be such in female as well as male representations.

8. The categories of masculine-feminine, relied on extensively in Boff's proposal, are pivotal in the analysis of mariology done by certain psychologists of religion. Drawing particularly on Jungian psychology, Ann Belford Ulanov, Joan Chamberlain Engelsman and others have contended that the religious power of symbols of the divine is weakened and distorted if a particular symbol system represses the feminine principle.[36] This repression has occurred within the image of God in the west, with debilitating effects especially upon women's consciousness and identity, although men also suffer loss of wholeness and vitality. By contrast, the symbolism of Mary functions to reveal the feminine in the Godhead (recall Jung's interpretation of the dogma of the assumption as paving the way for the recognition of the divinity of the Theotokos),[37] and to open up a correlative

psychic experience of deity. Even for those who do not find Mary a personally viable religious symbol, she nonetheless does represent the psychologically ultimate validity of the feminine principle, insuring a religious valuation of bodiliness, sensitivity, relationality, and nurturing qualities, such being prototypically feminine characteristics in the Jungian system. The symbol of Mary is necessary to balance the masculine principle in the deity which expresses itself in rationality, assertiveness, independence and taking charge.

A number of feminist thinkers have resoundingly rejected the Jungian category of the feminine, arguing that it is a patriarchal invention made on the basis of a profoundly dualistic anthropology which stereotypes women and constricts them to predetermined, private, politically powerless roles.[38] The point to note here, however, is that in this system of thought the symbol of Mary reveals what its adherents call the feminine dimension of the divine. Without this symbol, divine imagery is impoverished; with it, what has been excluded from participating in God, namely the feminine, finds a place and in turn becomes capable of revealing the divine. For our investigation, what can be retrieved from the Jungian approach, even if we find the masculine-feminine categories not viable, is the idea that much of what has been excluded from the image of God in classical theism can rightly be predicated of God (necessitating development in the doctrine of God), and that the figure of Mary is a resource for this development.

9. Using Jungian categories but within the framework of the social sciences, Andrew Greeley proposes in a similar vein that Mary is and should remain a symbol of the feminine component of the divine. According to his argument, the tradition of female deities arose historically from the conviction that God has feminine as well as masculine characteristics, a conviction born primordially from the experience of human sexual differentiation. An outstanding example in the world's tradition of female deities, Mary reveals the tender, gentle, comforting, reassuring—i.e. feminine—dimension of God. Greeley notes that the Protestant reformers were right in their perception that Mary had taken on a quasi-divine role in the Catholic tra-

dition, but wrong in judging that this detracted from the true worship of God. Her function is that of a "mysterion" who breaks open the experience of the Ultimate as "passionately tender, seductively attractive, irresistibly inspiring, and graciously healing."[39] Without that component, human insight into God is one-sided and incomplete. The author's living commitment to this insight is expressed in his lyric poetry:

> Mother, wife, muse, morning star
> A revelation of God's warming charms
> To a cold and bitter world. . . .[40]

Greeley's thesis presents many difficulties. In addition to his acceptance of stereotypes of what constitutes the so-called feminine, his grounding of this view of Mary in the experience of sexual differentiation limits its viability for the church as a whole. What are heterosexual women and homosexual men to make of an approach based on this figure's seductive attractiveness? Greeley's is a male construction (which he admits) which may work for heterosexual males or lesbian women (which limitation he doesn't seem to notice or try to overcome). Furthermore, as with Elizondo and Boff, there is the doctrinal and ecumenical difficulty that the person of Mary does function in a quasi-divine way which overshadows the priority of God. The other side of the latter problem is that the argument for keeping Mary in the role of revealing God's warming charms prevents the direct attribution of such appealing characteristics to God in her own right. There is, too, the added problem that the ideal feminine described by these authors (as by so much of the tradition) functions as an obstacle to real women's growth, preventing the integration of questioning intellect, capacity for righteous anger, and other characteristics of the mature personality. However, the valuable points which can be gleaned from this approach are the affirmation that the Marian tradition does carry important imagery of the divine, and the suggestion of what some of that imagery might be.

10. Tracing links between the figure of Mary and the image of God has not been limited to Roman Catholic theolo-

gians and historians. A number of Anglican scholars have explored this relation, finding in Mary a life-giving symbol of divine creativity and saving love which helps to correct Christianity's heavy masculine emphasis in the concept of God.[41] More startling, in view of the basic intuitions of the reformation, is a statement of a working group of German Lutherans officially engaged in studying Catholic mariology and Marian piety.[42] Their report describes Mary as a double-edged symbol within the faith of the church: she is a symbol of human faith and discipleship, and she also symbolizes the fact that God can be imaged with feminine and maternal characteristics. Noting how Marian devotion has consistently paralleled Mary to Jesus, these theologians seek to interpret positively what in the past they would have condemned as a distortion. The Marian phenomenon is to be attributed to humanity's desire for a maternal, mild, life-giving gestalt of God. The whole history of religions demonstrates this need, they affirm, and the original gospel could insinuate itself into its surrounding cultural milieu only by incorporating some feminine imagery. As Mary was the first human being to give a full response to God's word, so too as mother of God she becomes the "revelation of the feminine-maternal side of the being of God."[43] The Lutherans are quick to note the danger of Mary's divinization that could result, but nevertheless do identify her with a certain revelation, "*Offenbarung*," of God.

This position is reminiscent of that of Schillebeeckx, seeing the symbol of Mary disclosing something of God which the figure of Christ is incapable of modeling. While subject to the same critique of stereotyping the feminine and of limiting the capacity of female imagery to revealing only one "side" of God, its value lies in the acknowledgement of the figure of Mary as a bearer of revelation, and this from a group classically focused on the reality of revelation through Christ alone.

At the end of this survey of ten discrete positions on the question of Mary as a bearer of images of the divine, our initial hypothesis appears in a stronger light. Historians of the development of doctrine, Catholic theologians with a classical doctrinal interest, liberation and feminist theologians, thinkers in

the psychology of religion and the social sciences, and reforma-
tion-tradition theologians with ecumenical openness: all di-
versely affirm that Marian devotion and theology are sources of
understanding the holy mystery in female language and symbols. Certainly not all would agree that this phenomenon is due
to the patriarchal character of the dominant idea of God, nor
that there is pressing need to retrieve lost elements of the divine
kept safe in the Marian tradition and to reattribute them to
God's own reality. But all do acknowledge the function of the
figure of Mary in imaging the divine in a certain way not available in the predominant idea of God or Christ. It remains now
to see in an initial way just what the Marian tradition has to
contribute to an inclusive imaging of God.

FEMALE IMAGES FOR GOD

The holy mystery of God so transcends the capacity of
human concepts and finite images that no one of them alone or
even all taken together could ever capture or exhaustively express the divine reality. The reality of God springs forth beyond
and within all notions. This realization, and the intellectual
humility that it evokes in discussions of the question of God, has
usually been expressed in the Catholic tradition through the
doctrine of analogy, more usually in the Protestant traditions
through the idea of metaphor, and more recently in both traditions with the theory of symbol. We speak of God in finite words
which escape our own comprehension in arriving at their term.
But all words are not equally suitable to express the holy mystery. What words, then, should be used?

In classical theology perfections such as goodness and wisdom, drawn from the human world, considered transcendental
perfections according to philosophical analysis, and displayed
by the revealing God of the scriptures, were predicated of God.
Unquestioned by the great thinkers of the past, an ideological
bias, created by and supportive of patriarchal society, shaped
the image of God which accompanied this predication. God was
envisioned in the image of the ruling class, and spoken of as the
chief of all dominant males. Anything remotely reminiscent of

women was excluded from the pool of what could rightly refer to the being of God, for women were considered subordinate both in the realm of nature and that of grace (which situation would be corrected in the eschaton).[44] As was seen above, efforts by contemporary thinkers to redress the distortion in the inherited idea of God often begin with a positive evaluation of the "feminine" and a subsequent predicating of feminine attributes to God. The difficulty with many of these efforts, well-meaning as they are, is that they take no cognizance of the still-reigning patriarchal system of relationships, a system defined by male dominance and female subordination, within which their thought is shaped. Consequently, the "feminine" in God is allowed to appear only in limited references, as a partial aspect, or as a principle which mediates or tempers the strong power of God who remains imaged primordially as male. Even after the feminine is attributed to God, the male still reigns. The female never appears as icon of God in all divine fullness. By contrast, the perspective which sees both male and female created in the divine image and called to equal responsibility and dignity (Gen 1:26–29; Gal 3:28) finds both sexes equally capable and equally incapable of imaging the holy mystery. In fact, both are needed, as are images from the natural world, to prevent any one image from turning into an idol. In their similarities and differences the full range of creatures evokes the unfathomable depths of the mystery of God. In eliciting from the Marian tradition the rich imagery and language about the divine which it carries, I am operating within this latter perspective. What is found in the figure of Mary and attributed to God is not to be fitted into some dimension or aspect, but understood as primordially expressive of the being of God imaged as female. What then can be retrieved? Without claiming to be comprehensive, five elements present themselves as viable candidates for divine imagery.

The first and most obvious is the image of God as mother. The birthing and maternally caring metaphors which the Hebrew scriptures use to describe God's unbreakable love for the covenanted people have been concretized and carried forward in the figure of Mary.[45] Throughout the tradition she has been portrayed predominantly as the mother *par excellence,* caring and concerned, always ready to come to the aid of her children. Transferring this maternal language back to God enables us to see that God herself has a maternal countenance. All that is creative and generative of life, all that nourishes and nurtures, all that is benign, cherishes and sustains, all that is full of solicitude and sympathy originates in her. Maternal fruitfulness, care and warmth, and indispensable mother-love flow from God the Mother toward all creatures. All mothering on earth has its source in her. She exercises a maternity that does not leave us orphans. In a Sunday talk Pope John Paul I once spoke of God as our Father but even more as our Mother, who wants to love us even if we are bad.[46] The image has the capacity to release profoundly attractive characteristics of God long suppressed in a patriarchal system. Notice that what is overcome here is a popular concept of heavenly interaction modeled on a patriarchal household, in which a distant and judgmental God the Father is inclined to be approachable and more lenient through the intercession of Mary the mother on behalf of wayward children. Instead, maternity itself is equated of God equally with paternity, and female images of the creativity and caring intrinsic to healthy mothering may then evoke the reality of God.

Another, closely related element which can be found in the Marian tradition is that of divine compassion. Biblical studies have shown how the Hebrew word for mercy is linguistically rooted in the term for a woman's womb, and consequently evokes the idea of "womb-love" for the one whom a mother has carried and shaped from her own flesh.[47] Despite the New Testament's overwhelming witness that the mercy of God is made effectively present in Jesus Christ, and the symbolizing of that fact in such images as Jesus as the mother bird gathering her brood under her wing (Mt 23:37–39), the medieval split of the kingdoms of justice and mercy resulted in the Marian tradition being the primary bearer of this good news. In much preaching and piety Mary has been presented as more approachable than Christ, especially when one is conscious of human weaknesses. The classical Marian antiphon *Salve Regina,* for example, salutes Mary as "mother of mercy, our life, our sweetness and our hope"; to her the poor banished children of Eve send up their sighs and pray: "Turn then, most gracious advocate, thine eyes of mercy toward us." In the end Mary is asked to show us Jesus, but the form of the prayer itself casts her in the life-giving role of the merciful one. Returning this language to God to whom it properly belongs enables us to name the holy mystery as essentially and unfathomably merciful. God is the Mother of mercy who has compassionate womb-love for all her children. We need not be afraid to approach. She is brimming over with gentleness, loving-kindness and forgiveness, lavishing love and pity on the whole sinful human brood. Her judgment is true, most devastating to those who refuse the call for conversion to the same kind of mercy toward others: their self-righteousness is to no avail. Yet to the most ordinary as well as to the most blatant of wrong-doers who wish to repent, she is a true refuge of sinners. In addition to mercifully forgiving sin God consoles in all troubles and, in bending with care over those who suffer, is the true comforter of the afflicted.[48] It is not the case that God is essentially just with a justice which needs to be tempered by Mary's merciful intercession. Rather, compassion is primordially divine, as is suitably disclosed in the symbol of the merciful woman.

The Marian tradition has thirdly carried images of divine power and might in female form. In a statement reflective of personal experience but widely typical of western consciousness Dorothee Soelle has described male power as having something to do with "roaring, shooting, and giving orders,"[49] images of power-over which are implicit in most classical discussions of the omnipotence of the patriarchal God. On the other hand, after her long study of Marian legends and images, M. Jameson was moved to comment that in the depiction of and devotion given to Mary's gracious presence, "I have beheld an acknowledgement of a higher as well as gentler power than that of the strong hand and the might that makes the right. . . ."[50] In this case it is a strength which seeks to protect and to save, to liberate and to heal. The earliest known prayer of petition to Mary reflects this sense of primordial saving power: "We take refuge under the protection of thy compassion, O mother of

God. Do not neglect our prayers in our troubles, but free us from danger, thou who alone art pure (or revered), thou who alone art blessed."[51] These are phrases reminiscent of the psalms and of the petition to the Father to "deliver us from evil" in the prayer that Jesus taught. As the Marian tradition grew, so too did belief in Mary's protective power. There is a pervasive sense in the Marian cult that her power is not restricted by the demands of ecclesiastical law, nor bound by the power of Satan, nor even by the male god-figures of Father and Son to whom she is supposedly subject. She saves whom she loves if those in need but turn to her.[52] This is graphically illustrated by the widespread medieval iconography of the Madonna of the Protective Mantle. Under the umbrella formed by her draped, outstretched arms huddle a family, a religious order, a king, even a whole town's populace; there they find protection from evil which threatens, be it plague, war, temptation, or eternal judgment. Understanding all of this as primarily imagery of the divine unlocks the realization that the power of God is not destructive, aggressive or overbearing but operates wisely and justly in a form of advocacy for human beings. God's might is effective in breaking the stranglehold of evil and freeing those whom it has held in bondage, putting down the mighty from their thrones and exalting those of low degree (Lk 1:52). She powerfully seeks and succeeds in finding what is lost, as disclosed by the Lukan Jesus' imaginative parable of a homemaker searching for her lost coin (Lk 15:8–10). None can escape her saving grasp. This kind of power, carried in the imagery of a female figure of "might and mercy,"[53] of a woman who is mighty to save, is more accurately attributable to God's own being.

The immanence of God, so often underplayed in classical theism, is yet another element emphasized in the Marian tradition. In an effort to offset the distant, too-masculine God of the reformation, Paul Tillich developed the idea of God as the ground of being, a metaphor which symbolized the "mother quality of giving birth, carrying, and embracing, and, at the same time, of calling back, resisting independence of the created, and swallowing it."[54] In the Catholic tradition that function has partially fallen to the figure of Mary. Indeed, it has been Catholic experience that, as John Paul II tellingly observed, the eternal love of the Father manifested in history through the Son given for us "comes close to each of us through this Mother and thus takes on tokens that are of more easy understanding and access by each person."[55] This closeness of the love of God, this sense of the divine presence surrounding and pervading the creature, has been given striking expression in Gerard Manley Hopkins' poem "The Blessed Virgin Compared to the Air We Breathe":

> Wild air, world-mothering air,
> Nestling me everywhere . . .
> Minds me in many ways
> Of her . . .
> I say that we are wound
> With mercy round and round
> As if with air: the same
> Is Mary, more by name.
> She, wild web, wondrous robe,
> Mantles the guilty globe . . .
> And men are meant to share
> Her life as life does air . . .
> Be thou then, O thou dear
> Mother, my atmosphere . . .
> World-mothering air, air wild,
> Wound with thee, in thee isled,
> Fold home, fast fold thy child.[56]

The imagery of such insights refers most properly to the reality of God. So redirecting it enables us to realize that it is the wild Spirit who is our true atmosphere, who folds us fast. Most truly it is in her that we live and move and have our being (Acts 17:28). God the Spirit is closer to us than we are to ourselves. She holds fast to all who spring from her being, surrounds them, and continuously loves them into life. All that is awakens and sleeps, develops and decays in the presence of her holy love, and is finally enfolded into her eternal presence at the end. Rather than Mary being the figure who functions to make a distant patriarchal God close, immanence as well as transcendence is properly attributable to God's own being. This interiority of God to creation has been effectively evoked in the image of a woman, matrix of all that is gifted with life.

Finally, the understanding of God as source of recreative energy is one more element which can be drawn from the cult of Mary. "May is Mary's month" writes the poet Hopkins, and all that is swelling, bursting and blooming so beautifully does so under her aegis. Marian symbols of earth and water, vines, flowers, eggs, birds and young animals evoke her connection with fertility and the motherhood of the earth.[57] The theme of overturning the ancient sin and beginning again, so connected with her historic pregnancy, finds its parallel in the renewing of the earth. As Anselm wrote: "plenty flows from you to make all creatures green again."[58] Attributing this imagery directly to God allows us to affirm that it is God's own self who is the source of transforming energy among all creatures. She initiates novelty, instigates change, transforms what is dead into new stretches of life. Fertility is intimately related to her creative divine power. It is she who is ultimately playful, fascinating, pure and wise, luring human beings into the "more." As mover and encourager of what tends toward stasis, God herself is ever new and imaginative, taking joy in creating and recreating all that exists.[59]

CONCLUSION

Maternity with its nurturing and warmth; unbounded compassion; power that protects, heals and liberates; all-embracing immanence; recreative energy: thus is borne out the hypothesis that the Marian tradition is a fruitful source of female imagery of God.[60] Not just "dimensions" but ultimate metaphors for the divine mystery are available here. Received within a believing community that has let go of gender dualism (not difference) as a basic filter for viewing reality, each of these retrieved images has the power to contribute to a new naming and experiencing of the holy mystery.

Several cautions should be noted at this point. It is not the case that these characteristics exhaust the fullness and depth of women's reality. The life and experience of women, made in God's image and likeness, can generate many more images of the divine beyond what is found in the Marian tradition. Conversely, these are not the only images needed for the rehabilitation of the patriarchal idea of God. Others such as lover and friend, not easily found in the Marian tradition, need to be retrieved from other sources.[61] What has been pursued here is only one path among the many that need to be explored as we deconstruct and reconstruct theology toward genuine inclusiveness. Any claim to a total synthesis would be premature.

A further caution lies in the fact that with the exception of the medieval idea of Mary's saving power, even the images we have retrieved are open to the charge of being stereotypically feminine, of being instances of the "patriarchal feminine" which defines women in pre-conceived categories helpful to the male.[62] There is an obvious truth to this criticism, due to the fact that the Marian tradition has been shaped by the forces of a patriarchal history. Within androcentric thought structures, the figure of Mary became the locus around which clustered indispensable religious themes and symbols for which there was no room in the dominant image of God. Her symbol has thereby functioned as an icon of God, the "other face" of God within a patriarchal system. Realization of this state of affairs has undergirded the argument here that these themes and symbols should not now be transferred to God via the categories of "dimension" or "trait," for this would merely perpetuate the inherited, basically distorted system. Rather, each element that this exploration has turned up represents a missing or underdeveloped piece in our repertoire of references to God, and should be allowed to connote and evoke the whole of the divine mystery, in tandem with a plethora of other images.

This theological study has tested the hypothesis that the Marian tradition is a rich source of divine imagery, and found it a viable one. Maternity, female compassion, liberating power, intimate presence, and recreative energy—in a manner of speaking, Mary has treasured these things in her heart (Lk

2:19), awaiting the day when what has been guarded in her symbolism could find its rightful place in God again. For the renewal of the doctrine of God, for the growth in human dignity of real women made in her image and likeness, and for a properly directed theology of Mary within a liberating community of disciples, it would be well to allow this imagery to disperse beyond Mary, in the direction of the reality of the holy mystery of God.

Notes

1. "The Role of the Blessed Virgin Mary, Mother of God, in the Mystery of Christ and the Church," *Constitution on the Church (Lumen Gentium),* chapter 8, especially articles 50, 53, 62, 67, in *The Documents of Vatican II,* Walter Abbott, ed. (New York: America Press, 1966). See commentaries by Otto Semmelroth, "The Role of the Blessed Virgin Mary, Mother of God, in the Mystery of Christ and the Church," in *Commentary on the Documents of Vatican II,* Vol. 1, Herbert Vorgrimler, ed. (New York: Herder & Herder, 1967) 285–96; René Laurentin, *La Vierge au Concile* (Paris: Lethielleux, 1965); Karl Rahner, "Zur konziliaren Mariologie," *Stimmen der Zeit* 174 (1964) 87–101; Anne Carr, "Mary in the Mystery of the Church: Vatican Council II," in *Mary According to Women,* Carol F. Jegen, ed. (Kansas City: Leaven Press, 1985) 5–32; and Michael Schmaus' postconciliar synthesis of Marian theology in *Der Glaube der Kirche* Vol. 2 (Munich: Max Hueber Verlag, 1970) 657–97.

2. For this evocative metaphor of mining the Marian tradition I am indebted to Lawrence Cunningham, *Mother of God* (San Francisco: Harper & Row, 1982) 103. Obviously not all of Marian doctrine and devotion will yield fruit in this investigation: biblical, much patristic, and some contemporary expression (e.g. Mary as type of the church) do not present a Mary who bears images of God, except insofar as she, like all human beings, is *imago Dei.*

3. In the course of its fifty years this journal has consistently

presented studies of the Marian tradition which have reflected the contemporary state of discussion. Tracing the history of this publishing brings to light the shifting foci of mariology in the last half-century. Key articles include:

- William McGarry, "A Fundamental Principle in Mariology," 1 (1940) 396–411, and 2 (1941) 35–52;

- Paul Gaechter, "The Chronology from Mary's Betrothal to the Birth of Christ," 2 (1941) 145–70 and 347–68;

- Joseph Plumpe, "Some Little-Known Early Witnesses to Mary's *Virginitas in Partu*," 9 (1948) 567–77;

- Roland Murphy, "Allusion to Mary in the Apocalypse," 10 (1949) 565–73;

- Noel Ryan, "The Assumption in the Early English Pulpit," 11 (1950) 477–524;

- Alastair Guinan, "Our Lady as Intercessor for the Departed," 15 (1954) 416–30;

- Paul Palmer, "Mary in Protestant Theology and Worship," 15 (1954) 519–40;

- Bertin Farrell, "The Immortality of the Blessed Virgin," 16 (1955) 591–606;

- J. Crehan, "*Maria Paredros*," 16 (1955) 414–23;

- Christian Ceroke, "Jesus and Mary at Cana: Separation or Association?" 17 (1956) 1–38;

- E.J. Cuskelly, "Mary's Coredemption: A Different Approach to the Problem," 21 (1960) 207–20;

- James Hennesey, "Prelude to Vatican I: American Bishops and the Definition of the Immaculate Conception," 25 (1964) 409–19;

- Joseph Crehan, "The Assumption and the Jerusalem Liturgy," 30 (1969) 312–25;

- Raymond Brown, "The Problem of the Virginal Conception of Jesus," 33 (1972) 3–34;

- Joseph Fitzmyer, "The Virginal Conception of Jesus in the New Testament," 34 (1973) 541–75;

- Alan Clark, "The Virgin Birth: A Theological Reappraisal," 34 (1973) 576–93;
- Raymond Brown, "Luke's Description of the Virginal Conception," 35 (1974) 360–62;
- J.A. Saliba, "The Virgin-Birth Debate in Anthropological Literature: A Critical Assessment," 36 (1975) 428–54;
- Eamon Carroll, "Theology on the Virgin Mary: 1966–1975," 37 (1976) 253–89;
- Patrick Bearsley, "Mary the Perfect Disciple: A Paradigm for Mariology," 41 (1980) 461–504.

4. For scripture: Virginia Ramey Mollenkott, *The Divine Feminine: Biblical Imagery of God as Female* (New York: Crossroad, 1984); Phyllis Trible, *God and the Rhetoric of Sexuality* (Philadelphia: Fortress Press, 1978); Sandra Schneiders, *Women and the Word: The Gender of God in the New Testament and the Spirituality of Women* (New York: Paulist, 1986); Elisabeth Schüssler Fiorenza, "The Sophia-God of Jesus and the Discipleship of Women," *In Memory of Her: A Feminist Theological Reconstruction of Christian Origins* (New York: Crossroad, 1983) 130–40; Elizabeth Johnson, "Jesus the Wisdom of God: A Biblical Basis for Non-Androcentric Christology," *Ephemerides Theologicae Lovanienses* 61 (1985) 261–94.

   For tradition: Kari Elisabeth Børresen, "L'Usage patristique de métaphores féminines dans le discours de Dieu," *Revue théologique de Louvain* 13 (1982) 205–20; Caroline Walker Bynum, *Jesus as Mother: Studies in the Spirituality of the High Middle Ages* (Berkeley: University of California Press, 1982), and idem, ". . . And Woman His Humanity: Female Imagery in the Religious Writing of the Later Middle Ages," *Gender and Religion: On the Complexity of Symbols,* Caroline Walker Bynum, et al., eds. (Boston: Beacon, 1986) 257–88; Julian of Norwich, *Showings,* translation and introduction by Edmund Colledge and James Walsh (New York: Paulist Press, 1978).

   For theological discussion: see the comprehensive

survey by Anne Carr, *Transforming Grace: Christian Tradition and Women's Experience* (San Francisco: Harper & Row, 1988) 134–79; Sallie McFague, *Metaphorical Theology: Models of God in Religious Language* (Philadelphia: Fortress Press, 1982); Mary Daly, *Beyond God the Father: Toward a Philosophy of Women's Liberation* (Boston: Beacon, 1973); Rosemary Radford Ruether, "Sexism and God-Language: Male and Female Images of the Divine," in *Sexism and God-Talk: Toward a Feminist Theology* (Boston: Beacon Press, 1983) 47–71; Elizabeth A. Johnson, "The Incomprehensibility of God and the Image of God Male and Female," *Theological Studies* 45 (1984) 441–65; Gail Ramshaw Schmidt, "De divinis nominibus: The Gender of God," *Worship* 56 (1982) 117–31; Rosemary Haughton, "Is God Masculine?" in *Women in a Men's Church*, Virgil Elizondo and Norbert Greinacher, eds. (New York: Seabury, 1980) 63–70.

5. This and the following quote taken from Teilhard de Chardin's letters, quoted in Henri de Lubac, *The Eternal Feminine: A Study on the Poem by Teilhard de Chardin*, trans. by René Hague, (London: Collins, 1971) 126 and 125.

6. Hugo Rahner, *Greek Myths and Christian Mysteries*, trans. by Brian Battershaw (New York: Harper & Row, 1963) 13.

7. Jean Daniélou, "Le culte marial et le paganisme," in *Maria: Etudes sur la Sainte Vierge*, D'Hubert du Manoir, ed. (Paris: Beauchesne et ses Fils, 1949) 159–81.

8. For concrete examples, see Daniélou, 176; H. Leclercq, "Marie, Mère de Dieu," *Dictionnaire d'archéologie chrétienne et de liturgie* Vol. 10/2 (Paris: Librairie Letouzey et Ané, 1932) col. 1982–2043; Joan Chamberlain Engelsman, *The Feminine Dimension of the Divine* (Philadelphia: Westminster Press, 1979) 122–33; Rosemary Radford Ruether, "Mistress of Heaven," *New Woman, New Earth*, Ruether, ed. (New York: Seabury, 1975) 36–62; Marina Warner, *Alone of All Her Sex: The Myth and Cult of the Virgin Mary* (New York: Alfred Knopf, 1976), passim; J. Salgado, "Le culte marial dans le bassin de la Méditerranée, des origines au début du IV siècle," *Marianum* 34 (1972) 1–41; R.E. Witt,

"The Great Forerunner," *Isis in the Graeco-Roman World* (Ithaca, N.Y.: Cornell University Press, 1971) 269–81. Witt concludes his study of the influence of the goddess Isis on mariology with the observation that Christians should acknowledge that the roots of their religion were abundantly watered not just by the Jordan but also by the Nile (280).

9. Scholarly opinions about the Isis-Horus model for artistic depictions of Mary-Jesus range from possible to probable to certain. See M. Jameson, *Legends of the Madonna as Represented in the Fine Arts* (London: Longman, Brown, Green, Longmans, & Roberts, 1857); Rosemary Radford Ruether, *Mary—The Feminine Face of the Church* (Philadelphia: Westminster Press, 1977); Giovanni Miegge, *The Virgin Mary*, trans. by Waldo Smith (Philadelphia: Westminster Press, 1955) 75; Witt, 326 n.50; Engelsman, 59, 126–27. A negative opinion with regard to the particular pose of the nursing madonna is registered by V. Tran Tam Tinh, *Isis Lactans: Corpus des monuments greco-romains d'Isis allaitant Harpocrate* (Leiden: Brill, 1973).

10. A.J. Festugière, "A propos des arétalogies d'Isis," *Harvard Theological Review* 42 (1949) 209–34; J. Gwyn Griffiths, *The Isis Book* (Leiden: Brill, 1975). The praise of Isis may be compared with Marian praise in east and west—cf. *Akathistos Byzantine Hymn to the Mother of God*, Paul Addism, trans. (Rome: Mater Ecclesiae Centre, 1983); Donal Flanagan ed., *In Praise of Mary* (Dublin: Veritas Publications, 1975).

11. Emile Saillens, *Nos vierges noires: leurs origins* (Paris: Les Editions Universelles, 1945); Marie Durand-Lefebvre, *Etude sur l'origine des Vierges Noires* (Paris: G. Durassié, 1937); Leonard Moss and Stephen Cappannari, "In Quest of the Black Virgin: She Is Black Because She Is Black," in *Mother Worship: Theme and Variations*, James Preston, ed. (Chapel Hill, N.C.: University of North Carolina Press, 1982) 53–74; Emile Mâle, *L'art religieux du XII siècle en France* (Paris: 1922); Ilene Forsyth, *The Throne of Wisdom* (Princeton: Princeton University Press, 1972).

12. See Warner, 276 and 387 n.8; Moss and Cappannari, 61;

Eileen Power, "Introduction," in Johannes Herolt, called Discipulus, *Miracles of the Blessed Virgin Mary*, trans. by C. Bland (London: G. Routledge & Sons, 1928) xi.

13. Epiphanius, *Panarion* 79:4, 7; cf. Hilda Graef, *Mary: A History of Doctrine and Devotion* I (New York: Sheed and Ward, 1963) 70–73. Geoffrey Ashe, *The Virgin* (London: Routledge & Kegan Paul, 1976), develops the thesis that this sect with its attractive worship of Mary was a threatening rival to the developing Catholic Church.

14. See Jaroslav Pelikan, *The Growth of Medieval Theology* (Chicago: University of Chicago Press, 1978) 158–74; H.P. Ahsmann, *Le culte de la sainte Vierge et la littérature francaise profane du moyen âge* (Paris: Editions Auguste Picard, 1930); Etienne Delaruelle, *La piété populaire au moyen âge* (Torino: Bottege d'Erasmo, 1975); Walter Delius, *Geschichte der Marienverehrung* (Munich: E. Reinhardt Verlag, 1963) 149–70; Jean Leclercq, "Grandeur et misère de la dévotion mariale au moyen âge," *La liturgie et les paradoxes chrétiens* (Paris: Les Editions du Cerf, 1963) 170–204; Heiko Oberman, *The Harvest of Medieval Theology* (Cambridge, MA: Harvard University Press, 1963) 281–322, especially "Mariological Rules," 304–08.

15. E.g. Judith Martin, "Theologies of Feminine Mediation: Hindu and Christian," *Journal of Dharma* 6 (1981) 384–97.

16. Cf. Thomas Aquinas, *Summa Contra Gentiles*, Book 4, ch.11:19, Charles O'Neil, trans. (Garden City, N.Y.: Doubleday & Co., 1956); cf. John van den Hengel, "Mary: Miriam of Nazareth or Symbol of the Eternal Feminine," *Science et Esprit* 37 (1985) 319–33.

17. Other factors included the subjectivizing of spirituality with a concomitant personalizing of the history of salvation—Leo Scheffczyk, *Das Mariengeheimnis in Frömmigkeit und Lehre der Karolingerzeit* (Leipzig: St. Benno Verlag, 1959); the use of the principle of analogy to create for Christ a partner like unto himself (Oberman); and the practice of applying christological scripture texts to Mary (Graef).

18. Anselm of Canterbury, "Prayer to St. Mary (3)," in *The*

Prayers and Meditations of St. Anselm, trans. by Benedicta Ward (New York: Penguin Books, 1973) 121.

19. Psalm 96/97, in *The Mirror of the Blessed Virgin Mary and The Psalter of Our Lady,* trans. by Sr. Mary Emmanuel (St. Louis: B. Herder Book Co., 1932) 254.

20. Ibid. 294–95.

21. For this and the following examples see Jaroslav Pelikan, *Reformation of Church and Dogma (1300–1700)* (Chicago: University of Chicago Press, 1984) 38–50; and Graef, Vol. I, 241–322.

22. This sermon is not one of Bonaventure's, but its influence was due in no small part to the fact that it was long thought to be so—see Graef, 281–90.

23. Edward Schillebeeckx, *Mary, Mother of the Redemption,* trans. by N.D. Smith (New York: Sheed and Ward, 1964—originally 1954) 101–28.

24. Ibid. 113–114. For social analysis of devotion to Mary during this same post-tridentine period, see Barbara Corrado Pope, "Immaculate and Powerful: The Marian Revival in the Nineteenth Century," *Immaculate and Powerful: The Female in Sacred Image and Social Reality,* Clarissa W. Atkinson, et al., eds. (Boston: Beacon, 1985) 173–200.

25. He now considers this distinction almost meaningless—see *Christ: The Experience of Jesus as Lord,* trans. by John Bowden (New York: Seabury, 1980) 514.

26. Yves Congar, *I Believe in the Holy Spirit,* Vol. I, trans. by David Smith (New York: Seabury Press, 1983), esp. 159–66; René Laurentin, "Esprit Saint et théologie mariale," *Nouvelle Revue Théologique* 89 (1967) 26–42; Leon Cardinal Suenens, "The Relation That Exists Between the Holy Spirit and Mary," in *Mary's Place in Christian Dialogue,* Alberic Stacpoole, ed. (Wilton, CN: Morehouse-Barlow Co., 1982) 69–78; idem, *A New Pentecost?* Francis Martin, trans. (New York: Seabury, 1975) 196–211; Heribert Mühlen, *Una mystica persona: Die Kirche als das Mysterium der Identität des Heiligen Geistes in Christus und den Christen* (Munich: Schöningh, 1968) 461–94. For discussion of basic themes see also H. Manteau-Bonamy, *La*

Vierge Marie et le Saint-Esprit (Paris: Lethielleux, 1971); J.M. Alonso, "Mariologia y pneumatologia," *Ephemerides Mariologicae* 21 (1971) 115–25, and 22 (1972) 395–405; *Le Saint-Esprit et Marie*—three volumes of the *Bulletin de la Societé Francaise d'Etudes Mariales* (Paris: Lethielleux, 1968–70); and René Laurentin, "Bulletin sur Marie, Mère du Seigneur," *Revue des sciences philosophique et théologique* 60 (1976) 452–56, and 70 (1986) 119 n.122, with bibliography.

27. Leo XIII, *Iucunda Semper* #5, in *The Papal Encyclicals: 1740–1981,* Claudia Carlen, ed. (Wilmington, NC: McGrath Pub. Co., 1981); quotation from Vol. II, 356–57. See Mühlen, op. cit., for discussion and critique.

28. Elsie Gibson, "Mary and the Protestant Mind," *Review for Religious* 24 (1965) 397.

29. In Robert Murray, "The Holy Spirit as Mother," *Symbols of Church and Kingdom* (London: Cambridge University, 1975) 315. For contemporary expression of this idea, see Donald Gelpi, *The Divine Mother: A Trinitarian Theology of the Holy Spirit* (Lanham, MD: University Press of America, 1984).

30. Leonardo Boff, "Mary, Prophetic Woman of Liberation," in *The Maternal Face of God: The Feminine and Its Religious Expressions,* Robert Barr and John Diercksmeier, trans. (San Francisco: Harper & Row, 1987) 188–203; Virgil Elizondo, "Our Lady of Guadalupe as a Cultural Symbol: The Power of the Powerless," in *Liturgy and Cultural Religious Traditions* (Concilium 102), Herman Schmidt and David Power, eds. (New York: Seabury Press, 1977) 25–33; fourteen U.S. Hispanic bishops, "Pastoral Message of U.S. Hispanic Bishops," *Origins* 12 (1982) 145–52; Ernesto Cardenal, *The Gospel in Solentiname,* Vol. 1, D. Walsh, trans. (Maryknoll, NY: Orbis, 1978) 25–32. See also the Ph.D. dissertation of Andres Guererro, *The Significance of Nuestra Senora de Guadalupe and La Raza Cosmica in the Development of a Chicano Theology of Liberation* (Harvard University, 1983).

31. Earliest accounts of the apparition can be found in Donald

Demarest and Coley Taylor, eds., *Dark Virgin: The Book of Our Lady of Guadalupe* (Freeport, ME: Coley Taylor Inc., 1956); comparison is made by Alan Sandstrom, "The Tonantsi Cult of the Eastern Nahua," in Preston, ed. *Mother Worship*, 25–50.

32. Virgil Elizondo, "Mary and the Poor: A Model of Evangelizing," in *Mary in the Churches* (Concilium 168), Hans Küng and Jürgen Moltmann, eds. (New York: Seabury, 1983) 64. Whether this understanding in itself is helpful to the liberation of women is a disputed point; see Ena Campbell, "The Virgin of Guadalupe and the Female Self-Image: A Mexican Case History," in Preston, ed., *Mother Worship*, 5–24; Evelyn Stevens, "Marianismo: The Other Face of Machismo in Latin America," in *Male and Female in Latin America*, Ann Pescatello, ed. (Pittsburgh: University of Pittsburgh Press, 1973) 90–100; Mary DeCock, "Our Lady of Guadalupe: Symbol of Liberation?" *Mary According to Women* (note 1) 113–41; C.R. Boxer, *Mary and Misogyny: Women in the Iberian Expansion Overseas, 1415–1815* (London: Duckworth, 1975).

33. Leonardo Boff, *The Maternal Face of God*, 93. A number of commentators on Boff's hypothesis have noted its relation to the idea of his fellow Franciscan, Maximilian Kolbe, for whom Mary is the summit where the love of the Paraclete finds its expression, and is even in a sense "his" incarnation. See Boff, ibid. 96; and studies by H. Manteau-Bonamy, *La doctrine mariale du Père Kolbe: Esprit-Saint et Conception Immaculée* (Paris: Lethielleux, 1975); F. Villepelée, *Le Bienheureux Père M. Kolbe: L'Immaculée révèle l'Esprit Saint* (Paris: Lethielleux, 1974); James McCurry, "The Mariology of Maximilian Kolbe," *Marian Studies* 36 (1985) 81–97.

34. E.g. Jean Galot, "Marie et le visage de Dieu," *Marianum* 44 (1982) 427–38; Kari Børresen, "Mary in Catholic Theology," in *Mary in the Churches*, Küng and Moltmann, eds., 54–55; J.-M. Hennaux, "L'Esprit et le féminin: la mariologie de Leonardo Boff," *Nouvelle Revue Théologique* 109 (1987) 884–95, a discussion of Boff's popular version of

his thesis entitled *Je vous salue Marie*, C. and L. Durban, trans. (Paris: Cerf, 1986).

35. Elisabeth Schüssler Fiorenza, "Feminist Spirituality, Christian Identity, and Catholic Vision," in *Womanspirit Rising*, Carol Christ and Judith Plaskow, eds. (San Francisco: Harper & Row, 1979) 136–48.

36. See Ann Belford Ulanov, *The Feminine: In Jungian Psychology and in Christian Theology* (Evanston, IL: Northwestern University Press, 1971), esp. 314–34; Engelsman, *The Feminine Dimension of the Divine* (note 8), with extensive bibliography.

37. C.J. Jung, *The Collected Works*, Herbert Read et al., eds. (Princeton, NJ: Princeton University Press, 1969). See especially Vol. 11: 107–200 and 355–470, R. Hull, trans.

38. Rosemary Radford Ruether, "The Female Nature of God: A Problem in Contemporary Religious Life," in *God as Father?* (Concilium 143), Johannes B. Metz and Edward Schillebeeckx, eds. (New York: Seabury, 1981) 61–66; Naomi Goldenberg, "A Feminist Critique of Jung," *Signs* (Winter 1976) 443–49, and her unpublished dissertation at Yale University, *Important Directions for a Feminist Critique of Religion in the Works of Sigmund Freud and Carl Jung* (1976).

39. Andrew Greeley, *The Mary Myth: On the Femininity of God* (New York: Seabury, 1977), 13 and passim; also Victor Turner and Edith Turner, *Image and Pilgrimage in Christian Cultures* (New York: Columbia University Press, 1978) 161–62.

40. Ibid. 210. A similar note is sounded by Richard Rohr, who argues that in the face of the widespread absence of fatherly love and fidelity in the human world, Mary effectively mediates divine love: "The sad thing is that much of the world probably would never have been able to believe in a God who loves unconditionally, a God who loves warmly, a God who loves gently, if not for Mary. . . . Mary has been, in fact, a sign of salvation on a psychological level. I am not saying theologically she is the savior. I am not saying in any way she is God. Rather, I am saying she becomes the mediator for many people, a believable sign.

She could love me!"—in "The Church Without Mary,"
Mary, The Spirit, and The Church, Vincent Branick, ed. (New
York: Paulist, 1980) 20–21.

41. Thus John Macquarrie, "God and the Feminine," *The Way*
—Supplement 25 (1975) 5–13. See also A.M. Allchin, *The*
Joy of All Creation: An Anglican Meditation on the Place of
Mary (Cambridge: Cowley Pub., 1984).

42. Catholica-Arbeitskreis der VELKD, "Maria. Evangelische
Fragen und Gesichtspunkte. Eine Einladung zum
Gespräch," *Una Sancta* 37 (1982) 184–201.

43. Ibid. 191.

44. See Kari Elisabeth Børresen, *Subordination and Equivalence:*
The Nature and Role of Women in Augustine and Thomas
Aquinas, trans. by C. Talbot (Lanham, MD: University Press
of America, 1981); Rosemary Radford Ruether, "Misogy-
nism and Virginal Feminism in the Fathers of the Church,"
Religion and Sexism, ed. R.R. Ruether (NY: Simon and
Schuster, 1974) 150–83; Eleanor C. McLaughlin, "Equality of Souls, Inequality of Sexes: Women in Medieval Theology," *Religion and Sexism,* 213–66.

45. See Pss 17:8; 36:8; 57:2; 61:5; 91:4; and Is 42:14; 45:10;
46:3–4; 49:14–15; 66:12–13, for examples.

46. *Osservatore Romano,* (September 21, 1978) 2. Discussed by
Hans Dietschy, "God Is Father and Mother," *Theology Di-*
gest 30 (1982) 132–33, from *Reformatio* 30 (1981) 425–32.
Cf. the treatment of the metaphor God as Mother in Sallie
McFague, *Models of God: Theology for an Ecological, Nuclear*
Age (Philadelphia: Fortress, 1987) 97–123; and reflections
based on first-hand experience of maternity by Margaret
Hebblethwaite, *Motherhood and God* (London: Geoffrey
Chapman, 1984).

47. Phyllis Trible, *God and the Rhetoric of Sexuality,* 31–59. Recognition of such interpretation has begun to make its way
into official ecclesial documents. For example, John Paul
II, noting that the Hebrew term for "mercy" is rooted in
the term for "womb" which gives mercy the semantic
nuance of the love of a mother, writes that the Old Testament attributes to the Lord the feminine characteristics of

tenderness and readiness to forgive, and that the New Testament canticle of Zechariah "rather identifies God's mercy with a mother's love"; cf. the encyclical *Rich in Mercy* (Washington, DC: United States Catholic Conference, 1981) 56–58 n.52, and 59 n.61.

48. Both this and the preceding title are taken from the Litany of Loreto; see also the Akathistos Hymn for similar titles.

49. Dorothee Soelle, *The Strength of the Weak: Toward a Christian Feminist Identity*, trans. by Robert and Rita Kimber (Philadelphia: Westminster Press, 1984) 112.

50. M. Jameson, *Legends of the Madonna* (note 9) xix.

51. Translation from Miegge, 136. Dated from the late third or early fourth century, this prayer was published by C.H. Roberts, *Catalogue of the Greek and Latin Papyri*, Vol. III (Manchester: John Rylands Library, 1938) n.470. See analysis by Gerard Sloyan, "Marian Prayers," in *Mariology* Vol. III, J.B. Carol, ed. (Milwaukee: Bruce, 1960) 64–68.

52. Cf. Paule Bétérous, *Les Collections de Miracles de la Vierge en Gallo et Ibéro-Roman au XIII Siècle*, published as *Marian Library Studies*, Vols. 15–16 (Ohio: University of Dayton, 1983–84); and Herolt, called Discipulus, *Miracles of the Blessed Virgin Mary*.

53. Anselm, "Prayer to St. Mary (2)," in Ward, 110.

54. Paul Tillich, *Systematic Theology* III (Chicago: University of Chicago Press, 1963) 293–94.

55. John Paul II, *Redemptor Hominis* (Washington, DC: U.S. Catholic Conference, 1979) #22.

56. *A Hopkins Reader*, John Pick, ed. (Garden City, NY: Doubleday & Co., 1966) 70–73.

57. Hopkins, ibid. 56–57. See analysis of symbols which connect Mary with natural life by René Laurentin, "Foi et mythe en théologie mariale," *Nouvelle Revue Théologique* 89 (1967) 281–307.

58. "Prayer to St. Mary (3)," in Ward, 120.

59. See the extraordinary series of paintings and meditations by Meinrad Craighead, *The Mother's Songs: Images of God the Mother* (New York: Paulist Press, 1986).

60. The question arises: once relieved of bearing divine imag-

ery, what pattern should a theology of Mary now take? The direction has already been set by biblical scholarship's rediscovery of Mary as a believing disciple; by magisterial documents' emphasis on Mary as a woman of faith related to Jesus Christ and the pilgrim church (Vatican II's *Lumen Gentium;* Paul VI's *Marialis Cultus;* John Paul II's *Redemptoris Mater*); and by feminist and liberation theology's focus on Mary as a genuine woman, a poor woman of the people. The next step might well be an incorporation of these insights into a praxis-oriented theology shaped by categories of memory, narrative, and solidarity.

61. See Sallie McFague's trinitarian metaphor of God as mother, lover, and friend in *Models of God: Theology for an Ecological, Nuclear Age,* 97–180.

62. Cf. Rosemary Radford Ruether's trenchant analysis of this notion in "The Female Nature of God: A Problem in Contemporary Religious Life," *God as Father?* (note 38).

Reconstructing a Theology of Mary

Elizabeth Johnson

In the late twentieth century, a century which has witnessed so much wrenching violence and destruction of human life, Catholic theology on every continent has begun to grapple with the magnitude of massive public suffering in the light of the good news of the gospel. As diverse from each other as the resulting political and liberation theologies might be due to their varied cultural contexts and scholarly dialogue partners, one common factor which unites them is the emphasis given to the practical structure of the *logos* of Christian theo-logy. This is commonly expressed in the idea that in theology, praxis has a certain priority in relation to theory. What is developing here is a complex approach to theology which gives foundational importance to the church's critical and transformative activity in the face of unjust structures which dehumanize persons. This critical, transformative activity, or praxis, forms the matrix in which the truth of the gospel is brought anew to expression. In other words, this theological approach is basically convinced that the church must be about the business of the reign of God in order for its thought to be true.[1]

Intrinsic to this method of theologizing is the profound religious intuition that *vox victimarum vox Dei est*. Human beings live in a world patterned by powerful structures of domination and subordination, structures which can be seen as concrete mediations of the biblical "principalities and powers."

The institutional violence unleashed by these structures has hurt, degraded, and killed countless human persons, and has massively distorted the *imago Dei* in this world. In the face of this suffering, biblical testimony, from the exodus to the death and resurrection of Jesus with its promise of the future for all, proclaims that God is not neutral but rather sides with the poor, the oppressed, the "disappeared," the lost ones of history. In loving compassion God identifies with these "non-persons" and acts to save in multifaceted ways, on both the personal and the societal level, both here and hereafter.

The religious intuition of the immeasurable dignity of victims leads contemporary praxis-oriented theologies to highlight the practical and political significance of classical doctrines. Teaching about God, for example, is the most practical of all ideas, for as the infinite mystery of compassionate and liberating love, God wills the growth of all human beings toward genuine personhood in interdependent freedom, opposing whatever mars or destroys the divine image in women and men. Unjust structures may and do deny human beings the possibility of becoming subjects, but God sustains this as a serious option for all. Furthermore, the cross of Jesus Christ is the historical scandal whereby God identified with all the victims of history. This identification was not marked simply by a passive acceptance of suffering, but by an active love so great that death was transformed into fullness of life. Jesus' resurrection is hope for all, assuring a future especially for those who have been eliminated or victimized or ground down into non-persons. Belief in this God of the living and the dead, the God "who gives life to the dead and calls into being the things that do not exist" (Rom 4:17), thus has a critical and productive force. It challenges all believers to become genuine disciples, to follow the footsteps of the suffering, liberating messiah of God on a path which will inevitably bring them into the struggle for the good of all human beings. Praxis-oriented theology is generated by, accompanied by, and followed by personal and ecclesial commitment to God's cause as the cause of human well-being, especially focused on those who are being defeated in the quest for full humanity.

Grappling to express the Christian faith from this stance, praxis-oriented theology makes use of new conceptual tools with which to approach the Christian tradition. Predominant among these hermeneutical aids are the categories of memory, narrative, and solidarity. These are not decorative notions brought in to adorn the Christian proclamation which can be better understood by more abstract thought processes. Rather, they are basic categories of a practical fundamental theology, categories of human historical consciousness which are fundamentally important to doing the truth in love in the midst of a conflictual world. The three are indissolubly connected: memory and narrative provide the experience of solidarity with its cognitive status, while the practice of solidarity gives memory and narrative their practical character. Taken together, they are categories which prevent anyone from defining history as the history of the conquerors to the neglect of the little ones of the earth. As constitutive elements of praxis-oriented theology they function in an emancipatory way in the service of the suffering and the forgotten ones.

At the outset of this exploration I am making a wager that these categories can be fruitfully used in developing insight into a theology of Mary, and furthermore that they can also be used to bring discussion of Mary into one mainstream of contemporary theologizing.[2] To those ends, this study first investigates each category as it is fundamentally described and used in contemporary praxis-oriented theology. Then attention turns to their functioning in a theology of Mary and in understanding the presence of Mary in the life of the church in mission.

MEMORY

To reduce someone to the status of a non-person, to keep someone quietly in the situation of bondage, a dominating power must take away memory of an individual's personal history, ancestors, and traditions. The histories of human oppression reveal that destruction of memory is a typical maneuver of totalitarian rule. Only official history is allowed, and this tells the story of those who have triumphed and conquered, while the story of the defeated ones is repressed. On the other hand, personal and corporate identity is formed when repressed memory is aroused: witness the fact that every protest and rebellion is fed by the subversive power of remembered sufferings and freedoms. Thus, memory is a category which serves to rescue threatened or lost identity. Obviously, memory is not understood here in a nostalgic sense which bathes the past in a transfiguring light; nor is it perceived as having a reconciling function, bringing the challenge of the past into harmony with the misery of the present. Rather, it is an incalculable visitation from the past which energizes persons.[3] By evoking the sufferings and victories of the past it startles those who are despondent into movement. By lifting up the unfulfilled promise of past suffering it galvanizes in such persons an unquenchable hope that new possibilities coming out of the past can be realized now, at last. By remembering a future which is still outstanding it opens the way to protest and resistance. In any event, the future is opened up in a new way by the surplus of meaning carried in the act of remembering. Such eschatological memory operates as a practical, critical, even liberating category through which historical identity is forged.

Because this kind of remembering brings into view a future which is still outstanding, a certain measure of danger is connected with it. There is danger for those who dominate others and thus benefit from the status quo, for their position is called radically into question. In causing dangerous perceptions to dawn upon the oppressed, remembrance of the past threatens the social establishment, which does indeed seem perpetually to fear the subversive content of such recollections. There is also danger for those oppressed who become empowered by memory, for once their passivity is called into question the ensuing struggle for the future may be life-costing. For both groups memories of suffering and of historically-realized freedom break the stranglehold of what is currently held to be plausible, and call the present into question. Remembrance, then, is a way of detaching people from the given situation, a kind of "intervention" which interrupts the omnipotence of the given situation.[4] Even without reference to what is explicitly religious, such remembering breaks through the grip of prevailing consciousness in the light of the glimpsed future, shocks persons into awareness of the compromises they have made with the prevailing trends and banalities of society, and brings to light new possibilities. It is thus dangerous at a profound level. Especially in a situation of oppression when the victims rather than the victors become the subject of memory, tradition reveals its subversive power. Insofar as a certain relationship with the past is itself an option for a definite kind of future in which a better history is possible for those who suffer and die, are poor and without rights, those who remember from the vantage point of the defeated bind themselves to these critical memories and allow their lives to be determined by the latter's promise. It is not a comfortable existence.

In praxis-oriented theology, this kind of memory is seen as a fundamental form of expression of Christian faith. At the heart of the Christian faith is the *memoria passionis, mortis, et resurrectionis Jesu Christi,* a very definite memory of concrete suffering, injustice, violence, and death, and of God's victory through it which grounds the promise of future freedom for all. As with any critical memory, remembrance of the crucified and risen Jesus Christ is dangerous in a very particular way: "Who is close to me is close to the fire; who is far from me is far from the kingdom."[5] For those in the so-called first world, the memory of the passion and death of Jesus interrupts the triumphant hubris of modern society, consciously making room for the dark reality of sorrow and death. In that dark light the dominant image of the all-competent human being in perfect control of everything is challenged and provoked, while importance is given to those who have failed and been lost.

Furthermore, remembering the passion of Jesus brings into view the disadvantaged, those who, like him, have been destroyed in history. The descent into hell is an essential part of the *memoria passionis,* evoking the crucified Jesus' solidarity with the dead. Calling to mind Jesus Christ's resurrection gives birth to the realization that these dead, the vanquished and forgotten, have a future which is as yet unrealized, which is promised yet unknown, although it has already begun. The promise per-

tains in a special way to victims. True, the experience of suffering is universal; no one escapes sorrow and melancholy, pain,
the exigencies of finiteness, guilt and death. The resurrection
indeed gives hope to all people. Yet, in view of the particularity
of the cross, it is especially the suffering of victims, of those
oppressed by injustice, which comes to mind in the Christian
memoria passionis Jesu, along with anticipation of a liberating
future precisely for them. Consequently memory presses for
the transformation of political life. Negative consciousness of
suffering coupled with the eschatological surplus hidden in the
anamnesis of the cross works out in a practical way. The dangerous memory of Jesus acts as a stimulus toward praxis to overcome the suffering of present victims as history rolls on. In the
present confession of the church, the very definite *memoria
passionis* in solidarity with the defeated becomes a universal
category of rescue: the growth of living human subjects acting
and suffering in history, and ultimately even hope for the dead.

Narrative

The church's dangerous memory—of Jesus, of the suffering of history's victims, of the eschatological future—has an
intrinsically narrative structure.[6] In the widest sense, life itself
has the character of a story, and human experience is brought
to expression through narrative in a way impossible to abstract
thought. The story mode of discourse gives human beings a way
to discover and lay bare what the world is and how they exist
in it, helps them to shape and make sense of the world, and
enables them to articulate order in the fathomless mystery of
their lives and to maintain it in the face of the unexpected.
Especially in moments of crisis, narrative gives sharp focus to
the fundamental human questions in a situation. All this is
accomplished through the power of the telling of the tale itself.
One cannot sift out the moral of the story and relay it, flat and
colorless, and hope to have the same impact. Rather, the dis-
closive and transformative power of the story is grasped only
through the narrative itself, and through the interrelations between the story, the storyteller, and the listeners. As Robert

McAfee Brown has described the method of the holocaust survivor and witness Elie Wiesel:

> You want to know about the kingdom of night? There is no way to describe the kingdom of night. But let me tell you a story. . . . You want to know about the condition of the human heart? There is no way to describe the condition of the human heart. But let me tell you a story. . . . You want a description of the indescribable? There is no way to describe the indescribable. But let me tell you a story. . . .[7]

There is something intrinsic in human experience which demands narrative; stories are an original and indispensable way in which human beings articulate understanding and are challenged to action.

Insofar as the living, dangerous memory of the Christian tradition relates believers to the concrete, fathomless suffering of past human experience, with the intent of involving them as active subjects in the ongoing Christian story, narrative is not merely a useful aid but has an irreducibly central role in faith and theology. The paradigmatic narrative which Christians tell is the story of Jesus as the story of God with us. At the heart of every eucharistic liturgy is the narration of what he did the night before he died. The gospels themselves are confessing narratives of his life and destiny, telling the story of the deeds of his ministry in and through which the reign of God was arriving. They tell of his healings and exorcisms; his prayer of intimacy to Abba; his prophetic insistence on openness to the poor and the outcast; his scandalous table community with tax collectors and sinners; his confrontation with the secure and self-righteous; his own imaginative telling of stories; the cry of the respectable that this man is a drunk and a glutton, a despiser of sabbath and tradition, a breaker of social convention. Above all the gospels narrate his passion and death in the belief that his life received its ultimate vindication from the power of God. The Christian proclamation of this story takes place against an eschatological horizon: only when all the living and the dead are fulfilled in

God will the promise of the narrative be fulfilled and the story end. In the meantime, the story of Jesus now experienced as the Christ—a story of real suffering, active love, and exaltation—remains the dangerous and subversive story by means of which the Christian community tries to order and live out its life.

In the analysis of praxis-oriented theologians, narrative is not a simple concept but has multiple aspects.[8] There is, first of all, its self-involving aspect. By telling and listening to the Christian story, persons locate themselves in a cultural, histori-cal, religious tradition and allow its insights and challenge to shape their identity as human subjects. The ongoing plot of their own lives is joined to the continuing Christian story. This aspect of narrative, however, is far from simply a privatized concern with the well-being of the single self, for self-involve-ment in the story leads to transformative action. Undoubtedly one of the most evocative (and widely used) ways of illuminating this aspect of narrative is itself a story told by Martin Buber, who describes a rabbi's tale:

> My grandfather was paralysed. One day he was asked to tell about something that happened with his teacher—the great Baalschem. Then he told how the saintly Baalschem used to leap about and dance while he was at his prayers. As he went on with the story my grandfather stood up; he was so carried away that he had to show how the master had done it, and he started to caper about and dance. From that moment on he was cured. That is how stories should be told.[9]

That is how the story of Jesus should be told, so that Christians become what they tell in the telling, to practical and critical effect. The narrative changes the persons who hear it and lures them into the way of discipleship, into the *imitatio Christi*.

There is, consequently, a practical and pastoral aspect to the story. Narrative is the language of the interruption of the system. By means of it persons can resist manipulation, for telling dangerous stories calls present socially-determined ar-rangements into question and presses toward new situations which do not simply reproduce current oppressive factors. Such stories are directed against systems which make the human person as subject disappear. They involve persons in liberating collective historical memories, and intrinsically turn them toward innovative praxis in the social order.

Christian narrative, thirdly, has a theological aspect, since it is a medium which mediates the experience of salvation within the historical experience of suffering. Rational argument breaks down in face of the surd of excessive human suffering, whereas story enables the touch of grace present in such experience to be thematized. When rational analysis and metaphysical discourse have offered the wisdom of their cool logic, the surplus of what is still to be said is uttered in stories. This is not done in such a way, however, as to bring intelligibility to the suffering, or to give prematurely a sense of how it all works out. The experience of suffering has generated in the classic tradition an awareness of the apophatic dimension of faith expression: silence, simplicity, iconoclasm. Refusing to trivialize tragedy, narrative finds its home in this dimension, birthing hope and resistance in the midst of darkness. Its evocative telling of the memory of the passion, death, and resurrection of Jesus Christ is a mediation of salvation.

SOLIDARITY

This category rounds off the trio of forms underlying praxis-oriented theology by providing memory and narrative with the basis of their practical structure. In a broad sense all human persons are related to all others who have lived, do live, or will live on the face of the earth (or elsewhere) as members of the one human race. In classical Catholic theology this realization undergirds the doctrines of original sin and of the universality of redemption. As shaped by contemporary political consciousness, however, the term has come to signify more than simply a generic relationship. Rather, it connotes a vital union of interests within a group, a genuine community of desires, expectations and goals. In this sense it is used by praxis-oriented theology as a category with both mystical and political dimensions.[10]

As the one whose very identity is determined by total identification with the being of God and with suffering humanity,
Jesus Christ is at the center of Christian solidarity. The narrative remembrance of Jesus' scandalous solidarity with the poor
and outcasts, even with the dead, as a way of bringing about the
reign of God finds its ultimate religious significance when this
solidarity is confessed as the mediation of God's own solidarity
with suffering humanity. Precisely here the Christian idea of
God receives its specificity: in the realization that the partisanship of Jesus toward those marginalized by power systems
makes present the partiality of God toward those historically
deprived of love and justice, and that the kenosis and humilia-
tion of the Son mediates the redemptive solidarity of God with
the poor and oppressed victims of history. Such community is,
therefore, the way of human salvation. Rejecting this solidarity
with the poor is excluding ourselves from where God is most to
be found. Entering into this solidarity puts us on a path determined not by self-interest but by interest in the ones who suffer;
we are drawn ever further into the praxis of partisanship in
imitatio Christi.

Solidarity, therefore, does not mean a community of interest with just one other beloved person in an "I-Thou" relationship. Nor does it involve only common feeling with those in our
immediate neighborhood, economic bracket, or cultural world.
It is not optimistic sympathy for the less fortunate, nor pessi-
mistic perception of them as a collectivity. It involves instead a
personal partnership of desires and interests with those in
need, with those most in need, perhaps causing us loss. In vital
community one enters into common reflection and action
against the degradation which so defaces human persons, and
does this with the sense that these human persons are part of
oneself. The universality of this category, furthermore, is
shown in the fact that it includes not only the living. Rather, it
involves an alliance with the dead, especially with those who
have been overcome and defeated in history. The narrative
memory of the dead creates a solidarity backward through time,
which emphasizes the common character of human destiny. It is
thus a category of help, support and togetherness, by means of

which the dead can be affirmed as having a future, and living persons who are oppressed and acutely threatened can be raised up toward becoming genuinely free, and leaders and persons more well-off can enter into the path of conversion in the practical following of Christ. This historical anamnetic solidarity between the living and the dead breaks the grip of dominating forces and empowers transformative praxis toward a fulfilling future for *all,* guaranteed only when the value of the most despised is assured.

After a season of forgetting, the categories of memory, narrative and solidarity drawn from the wellsprings of scripture and liturgy are being pressed again into the service of Christian reflection by contemporary praxis-oriented theology. Based on vital solidarity, the narrative remembrance of Jesus and of the suffering of the oppressed articulates and mediates the experience of saving grace in the midst of the disasters of history. Inevitably critical of the banality of evil, this approach orients believers to praxis, to action on behalf of the reign of God in the face of a godless world. Protest, resistance, and hope in God who raises the dead become the way of life for the church, that community which cherishes and publicly witnesses to the dangerous memory of Jesus as God's presence and activity in this world.

What, then, of Mary? Is she included in the living solidarity of those who have suffered in history? Is her memory in any way dangerous? Does her story turn believers to thirst for justice? How might the tradition about this preeminent member of the church, honored as mother of God, come to expression in the categories of praxis-oriented theology? I propose to engage here in a kind of "thought experiment"[11] to explore these questions. The attempt is not exhaustive of all possible aspects of the Marian tradition, but engages several which may serve as examples for the rest.

MARY IN PRAXIS-ORIENTED THEOLOGY

The Second Vatican Council's main teaching on Mary is structured in *Lumen Gentium,* chapter 8, according to the rubric of her participation within the twofold mystery of Christ and the church.[12] In describing her relation to Christ, the council document uses narrative, telling the story of Mary's participation in the events of salvation history focused on Jesus Christ. Her participation in the mystery of the church is developed through the idea of Mary as one with the church, indeed a type of the church, living within the community as a preeminent member who reflects to all believers what they are called to be. Thus in a formal way, the categories of memory, narrative and solidarity are already used in the conciliar text. Within the framework of praxis-oriented theology, these categories assume a critical force.

First of all, it is established that Christian believers are in solidarity with Mary in a vital community of interests and goals which reaches backward and forward in time. She is one of those politically insignificant ones who have gone from this earth, but whose journey through life witnesses to the immense value of each human person. The whole Christian tradition of the saints provides a context in which this solidarity with Mary can be understood. The saints and martyrs of the Christian tradition powerfully lived out, each in his or her own way, the ongoing story of Jesus Christ in history.[13] All of them entered upon the path of struggle on behalf of the reign of God in the situations in which they found themselves. In spite of their sinfulness and personal quirks, there is not one story of these human followers of Christ in which the elements of suffering and goodness toward others do not shine through. These persons are not among the forgotten dead. Rather, the tradition of the saints in the church keeps the memory of their lives alive within *the* dangerous memory of Jesus, as particular versions of the praxis of the gospel, as narratives spelling out in countless ways the approach of grace amid the struggle. In the Christian remembrance of its members who were publicly ignored, derided or executed, the memory of all whom the world has scorned is lifted up. In the story of Christian leaders who broke through patterns of domination by acts of compassion and justice, the power of present oppressors is judged. Undergirded by the doctrine of the communion of saints, anamnetic solidarity with the saints warms, challenges, and cheers believers on their own way in the present moment of history.

Uniquely among these saints whom the church remembers, to practical and critical effect, is the person of Mary, the mother of Jesus, the mother of God. Within the narration of the dangerous memory of Jesus, the community of disciples tells the story of this woman's tears and her joy in God, finding itself thereby impelled toward similar growth in genuine personhood and faith. This experience of anamnetic solidarity does not exclude but rather presupposes a commonality of humanity with her. Mary and all believers share experiences of suffering and mutual hope in God for a better future. At the same time, the way in which the biblical authors portray her free participation in God's work of salvation by mothering the messiah and by her ongoing hearing of the word of God makes her story unique among the stories Christians tell. Awareness of solidarity with Mary in a community of faith which remembers and tells unsettling stories, of which hers is one, may well be an effective rubric with which to begin and to situate an understanding of Mary within praxis-oriented theology.

More concretely, how is the memory of Mary to be narrated? What will come to the fore within the horizon of praxis-oriented theology? Within the context of her being a most faithful disciple, Mary can be remembered in at least five different ways: as a poor member of the people, as an "outsider," as a victim of violence, as a prophet of justice, and as a woman.

1. Politically Mary of Nazareth was part of a conquered nation oppressed in countless ways by an occupying foreign power. Her socio-economic status situated her not among the elite but among the relatively poor hard-working village people in first century Palestine. As a homemaker, mother, and wife she in all likelihood did not receive a formal education. In terms of the structures of religious authority she was excluded from any leadership role in temple or synagogue. Here, then, is not one of the powerful ones of the earth, but in civil and religious socio-political terms an insignificant rural woman. She is not an ideal beautiful queen as the medieval courtly singers envisioned her, but is more like the maids of their palace kitchens or the

peasant women of their domains.[14] The memory of Mary as of
low estate creates solidarity with downtrodden peoples today.
The publicly powerless and excluded can identify with her and,
glimpsing a future opening up for themselves in the story of the
great things God has done for her, respond to the call of God
with critical praxis on their own behalf.

2. The gospel of Matthew gives the memory of Mary a
further depth in its infancy narrative. Here Mary is introduced
as the last and most crucial link in a long genealogical chain,
wherein four foreign and/or sinful women—Tamar, Rahab,
Ruth, the wife of Uriah—enter into the history of the messianic
line. Like the other women of the genealogy, Mary is an
"outsider":

> In Matthew's account she becomes a member of the
> Davidic family only through her espousal to Joseph.
> And the Gospel throws a mantle of suspicion and
> abuse around her as it did with the other "foreigners"
> too; because she is with child prior to her espousal,
> Joseph, a just and compassionate man, decides he
> must divorce her quietly. But Joseph learns in a dream
> what the Gospel has already told the reader: Mary is
> with child by the Holy Spirit (1:18–19). Once again
> God has worked in an unexpected and extraordi-
> nary way.[15]

Mary is thus an outsider brought in to the center of the story by
the power of God, the unexpected "non-person" who brought
the messiah to life. In this context the virginal conception of
Jesus as presented in Matthew is, at the most profound theological level, an insight into the strange patterns of history: God
working to bring about salvation through people and circumstances that secure and self-satisfied human beings tend to ignore or disparage. Narrative remembrance of *this* Mary
rearranges one's vision of what is possible despite hardened
historical "givens" and turns "outsiders" toward action on behalf of their own dignity.

3. The *memoria passionis Jesu* also contains the memory of the suffering of Mary related to the cross. She lost her son not to death caused by illness or accident (sorrow enough in itself), but to a cruel and bloody death brought about by public execution. The violence of his death victimized her as well, as the mothers of La Playa, Argentina, and mothers of any victims of political violence could attest. She suffered the anguish of grief, and of the pain of oppression as occupying soldiers crucified her child. In the light of the holocaust one Jewish scholar has reflected that Mary's suffering must be seen in the specific context of the history of Jewish suffering through the centuries. It ennobles rather than profanes her memory to realize that Mary is precisely a sorrowful Jewish mother, one in a long line of countless Jewish mothers who have lamented their cruelly murdered Jewish children.[16] We tell of her mourning for her dead, murdered, innocent son in solidarity with all human suffering, and especially with the particular and concrete pain of mothers, the life-givers of the race. The narrative of this pain gives voice to the suffering of all those who grieve out of love for another destroyed by unjust powers, and gives rise to the critical stance which says: it should not have happened; it must not happen again.

4. But Mary is not simply a poor woman, an "outsider," a sorrowful victim of the violence of unjust powers. As depicted by Luke, she also proclaims the reality of God's justice with unflinching strength. In the great tradition of Hannah, Deborah, Miriam, Judith, and the unnamed mother of the seven sons in 2 Maccabees, she sings the song of God's justice, toward her and all the oppressed of the earth. The Magnificat, eloquently called by E. Schillebeeckx "A Toast to God,"[17] is a hymn of liberation, fiercely on the side of the oppressed, and fearlessly indicating the powerful who abuse those considered "non-persons":

God has shown strength with his arm . . . scattered the proud in the imagination of their hearts . . . put down the mighty from their thrones . . . exalted

> those of low degree . . . filled the hungry with good
> things . . . sent the rich away empty . . . (Lk
> 1:51–53).

This spirit of liberating justice pervades the entire ministry of
Jesus, who was sent to "proclaim release to the captives and
recovering of sight to the blind, to set at liberty those who are
oppressed" (Lk 4:18–19). In the spirit of her son, the song of
Mary proclaims the terrible judgment of God against the oppressors in the surpassing victory of those who know poverty,
weakness, suffering. Remembering Mary as the woman of justice, as the "Mirror of Justice" in the words of the Litany of
Loreto, stimulates the poor and those in solidarity with them to
work for bread, housing, and equal rights. This relation between *memoria Mariae* and the praxis of justice is especially clear
in the experience of contemporary Latin America.[18] The indigenous devotion to Our Lady of Guadalupe in Mexico, for example, indicates how the memory of Mary is held in tandem with
concern for the poor, and increasingly turns those who cherish
that memory toward critical praxis.[19] In the light of her song
those who are "lowly" or victimized by unjust oppression embrace the goal of truly living like persons of worth, rejoicing in
God and having that joy mediated through enjoyment of life.
With its extraordinary paradox of joy and pain the Magnificat
continues its powerful witness in the midst of the bloody struggle for justice. As one of the people, Mary reveals the Spirit of
God actively at work among the people, which becomes an
impetus for resistance and struggle against the sacrilege of their
degradation.

5. In every social class and political circumstance, women
as a whole are ranked below men. When this social discrimina-
tion is combined with racial and economic bias, women truly
become the oppressed of the oppressed. In the remembrance
of Mary throughout the whole Christian tradition, whatever
else may have been forgotten it has never been overlooked that
historically she is of the female gender. Precisely as a woman
her story may resonate with those of other women with whom

she is in solidarity through the strong bonds of sisterhood. While the form of praxis-oriented theology known as feminist theology has been generally critical of the way in which traditional androcentric thinking has distorted the memory of this woman, the approach through memory, narrative and solidarity may well restore the critical power of tradition about her.[20]

In her own Lukan words she is a lowly woman who has been lifted up by God to great things. She can be remembered in part: as a young woman who coped well with an extraordinary situation (the annunciation), having the good sense to question a heavenly messenger before making any decision and the wits to realize the implications of his answer; as a betrothed woman who at considerable personal risk courageously gave free and responsible consent to the call of God—and did so on her own initiative, without consulting male authority figures; as a traveling woman who left home in haste to seek the companionship of her "kinswoman" Elizabeth who was also amazingly filled with a new life; as a pregnant woman inspired by the Spirit of God to burst into prophecy about the greatness of God who liberated the poor; as an oppressed woman following the orders of an occupying military power which necessitated her giving birth far from home and without adequate provision; as a refugee woman fleeing with her family from the murderous intent of a jealous ruler; as a married woman collaborating with her husband in raising their precocious child and speaking for them both in the temple when their child seemed to get out of line; as a celebrative woman arranging for more wine at a wedding feast; as a mature woman who was not defined simply by childbearing but more profoundly by the way in which, as a disciple, she heard the word of God and acted upon it; as a courageous woman who bore the grief of the violent, destructive death of her son, not letting it destroy her; as a prayerful woman, again away from home as part of the community of disciples of women and men waiting for the gift of the Spirit of the risen Christ. Paul VI named Mary "truly our sister, who as a poor and humble woman fully shared our lot."[21] The solidarity of sisterhood with such a woman may turn oppressed women away from their common denigrating lack of self-esteem and passive acceptance of marginalization and toward critical praxis on behalf of personhood. The impetus is there.

The church is the bearer of the tradition of the dangerous memory of the freedom of Jesus. In the view of praxis-oriented theology, ecclesial public dogmas are formulae related to this memory which spell out, at various points in history, the knowledge born of actively living within the power of that dangerous memory.[22] The dogmas of Mary's freedom from original sin (immaculate conception) and of her eschatological victory in Christ (assumption) find vital interpretation within this framework. The former celebrates God's victory over the powers and principalities of this world as this woman comes into existence. In her very being through the mercy of God in Christ the grip of the evil one (the serpent of Genesis 3) is broken. The latter dogma recognizes that God's creation of the new heaven and new earth, inaugurated in the resurrection of Jesus, comes to further fruition in this woman. In her very person she participates in the new life promised to the human race through the word of the cross. Both dogmas take very seriously that life and death are a struggle, that the forces of evil are enormous, and that only by the power of God can anyone ultimately prevail. Each recognizes the critical distance that history still has to travel before salvation is complete, at the same time that each revitalizes hope in the ongoing power of God operating in human persons, overcoming the forces of evil and renewing the face of the earth. Amid the constant hostility and untold suffering of history, the narrative memory of these dogmas reminds the church of the undaunted power of this woman, free in her love for God and others through the power of grace, and finding ultimate victory. They can be remembered as prophecy in the midst of the history of suffering.

Many other aspects of the Marian tradition may be retrieved, to practical and critical effect, within the perspective of praxis-based theology. This tradition is a rich deposit of memories about a woman whose life-story as one of the poor ones of the earth was closely interwoven with the story of God actively bringing salvation, liberation, and deliverance in history. The categories of memory, narrative, and solidarity function as a hermeneutical key unlocking the treasure of that tradition and impelling it toward alliance with the struggle for justice. It can indeed be dangerous to remember her, who herself remained mindful of the great things God had promised and begun to do, pondering them in her heart (Lk 2:19).

Notes

1. It is not my intention to give a comprehensive account of praxis-oriented theology, nor to discuss attendant questions such as its relation to critical theory. Rather, I wish to draw attention to its main characteristics in a way simply sufficient to set the context for a new consideration of Mary.

   For background, see: Richard Bernstein, *Praxis and Action: Contemporary Philosophies of Human Activity* (Philadelphia: University of Pennsylvania Press, 1971), and *Theory and Practice: History of a Concept from Aristotle to Marx* (South Bend, IN: University of Notre Dame Press, 1983); Rebecca Chopp, *The Praxis of Suffering: An Interpretation of Liberation and Political Theologies* (Maryknoll, NY: Orbis, 1986); Francis Schüssler Fiorenza, "Political Theology and Liberation Theology: An Inquiry into Their Fundamental Meaning," in *Liberation, Revolution and Freedom: Theological Perspectives,* Thomas McFadden, ed. (NY: Seabury, 1979), 3–29; Gustavo Gutierrez, *The Power of the Poor in History,* trans. Robert Barr (Maryknoll, NY: Orbis, 1983); Johannes B. Metz, *Faith in History and Society,* trans. Davis Smith (NY: Seabury, 1980); Jürgen Moltmann, *The Crucified God,* trans. R. Wilson and J. Bowden (NY: Harper & Row, 1974); Jon Sobrino, *The True Church and the Poor,* trans. Matthew O'Connell (Maryknoll, NY: Orbis, 1984); David Tracy, *The Analogical Imagination* (NY: Crossroad, 1981), 390–404.

2. For the notion of making a wager as a way into and beyond

the hermeneutical circle, see Paul Ricoeur, *The Symbolism of Evil*, trans. Emerson Buchanan (Boston: Beacon Press, 1969), 347–57.

3. See J.B. Metz, *Faith in History and Society*, especially the discussion of memory in the essays "The Dangerous Memory of the Freedom of Jesus Christ," 88–99; "The Future in the Memory of Suffering," 100–118; and "Memory," 184–199.

4. See Metz, *Faith in History and Society*, 193–94, paraphrasing a favorite insight taken from Herbert Marcuse, *One-Dimensional Man* (Boston: Beacon Press, 1964).

5. A non-canonical word of Christ transmitted by Origen; see Metz, "Theology Today: New Crises and New Visions," *Proceedings of the Catholic Theological Society of America* 40 (1985), 11. Metz judges danger to be a basic category of the experience of Jesus, though for the most part Christian tradition has disregarded this.

6. See Stephen Crites, "The Narrative Quality of Experience," *Journal of the American Academy of Religion* 39 (1971), 291–311; Johannes B. Metz, "A Short Apology of Narrative," in *The Crisis of Religious Language* (Concilium Vol. 85), J.B. Metz and J.P. Jossua, eds. (NY: Herder & Herder, 1973), 84–96; Paul Ricoeur, "The Narrative Function," in *Hermeneutics and the Humane Sciences*, trans. and ed. by J.B. Thompson (NY: Cambridge University Press, 1981), 274–305; Terrence Tilley, *Story Theology* (Wilmington, Del.: Michael Glazier, 1985); David Tracy, *The Analogical Imagination* (NY: Crossroad, 1981), 275–81; Brian Wicker, *The Story-Shaped World* (London, 1975). Important for this discussion is insight into the cognitive status of narrative discourse: see Nicholas Lash, "Ideology, Metaphor and Analogy," in *The Philosophical Frontiers of Christian Theology*, ed. by B. Hebblethwaite and S. Sutherland (Cambridge: Cambridge University Press, 1982), 68–94; Michael Goldberg, *Theology and Narrative: A Critical Introduction* (Nashville: Abingdon, 1982).

7. Robert McAfee Brown, *Elie Wiesel: Messenger to All Human-*

ity (Notre Dame, IN: University of Notre Dame Press, 1983), 6–7.

8. See especially Metz, *Faith in History and Society*, 205–18; also Edward Schillebeeckx, *Jesus: An Experiment in Christology*, trans. by H. Hoskins (NY: Seabury, 1979), 77–80; and Harald Weinrich, "Narrative Theology," in *The Crisis of Religious Language* (Concilium Vol. 85), 46–56.

9. Schillebeeckx, *Jesus*, 674.

10. See Francis Schüssler Fiorenza, "Critical Social Theory and Christology: Toward an Understanding of Atonement and Redemption as Emancipatory Solidarity," in *Proceedings of the Catholic Theological Society of America* 30 (1975), 63–110; Matthew Lamb, *Solidarity with Victims* (NY: Crossroad, 1982), and "Christian Spirituality and Social Justice," *Horizons* 10 (1983), 32–49; Johannes B. Metz, *Followers of Christ*, trans. by Thomas Linton (NY: Paulist Press, 1978), and "Solidarity," in *Faith in History and Society*, 229–37; *The Mystical and Political Dimension of the Christian Faith* (Concilium Vol. 96), ed. by C. Geffré and G. Gutierrez (NY: Herder & Herder, 1974); Helmut Peukert, *Science, Action, and Fundamental Theology*, trans. J. Bohman (Cambridge, Mass.: MIT Press, 1984).

11. For the idea of a thought experiment in theology, see Sallie McFague, *Metaphorical Theology* (Philadelphia: Fortress Press, 1982).

12. Walter Abbott, *The Documents of Vatican II* (NY: America Press, 1966). See René Laurentin's description of the debates behind the document in *La Vierge au Concile* (Paris: Lethielleux, 1965).

13. Contemporary discussion of the saints includes Lawrence Cunningham, *The Catholic Heritage* (NY: Crossroad, 1983); William Thompson, *Fire and Light: The Saints and Theology* (NY: Paulist, 1987), and *The Jesus Debate* (NY: Paulist, 1985), 299–342; Gustavo Gutierrez, *The Power of the Poor in History*, 89, 194–99; Elizabeth Johnson, "May We Invoke the Saints?" *Theology Today* 44 (1987), 32–52. See also Karl Rahner's essays in *Theological Investigations:* "The

Church of the Saints," Vol. 3 (Baltimore: Helicon Press, 1967), 91–104; "Why and How Can We Venerate the Saints?" Vol. 8 (NY: Herder & Herder, 1971), 3–23; "All Saints," Vol. 8, 24–29.

14. Point made by John L. Mackenzie, "The Mother of Jesus in the New Testament," in *Mary in the Churches* (Concilium Vol. 168), ed. by Hans Küng and Jürgen Moltmann (NY: Seabury Press, 1983), 9.

15. Donald Senior, "New Testament Images of Mary," *The Bible Today* 24 (1986), 145–47; see this article for the theological interpretation which follows.

16. David Flusser in *Mary: Images of the Mother of Jesus in Jewish and Christian Perspective*, with Jaroslav Pelikan and Justin Lang (Philadelphia: Fortress Press, 1986), 7–16.

17. Edward Schillebeeckx, *God Among Us: The Gospel Proclaimed*, trans. John Bowden (NY: Crossroad, 1983), 20–26.

18. See Leonardo Boff, "Mary, Prophetic Woman of Liberation," *The Maternal Face of God*, trans. R. Barr and J. Diercksmeier (San Francisco: Harper & Row, 1987), 188–203; Virgil Elizondo, "Mary and the Poor: A Model of Evangelizing," in *Mary in the Churches* (Concilium Vol. 168), 59–65; Eduardo Hoornaert, "Models of Holiness Among the People," in *Models of Holiness* (Concilium Vol. 129), ed. by C. Duquoc and C. Floristan (NY: Seabury Press, 1979), 36–45.

19. See Virgil Elizondo, "Our Lady of Guadalupe as a Cultural Symbol: The Power of the Powerless," in *Liturgy and Cultural Religious Traditions* (Concilium Vol. 102), eds. H. Schmidt and D. Power (NY: Seabury Press, 1977), 25–33.

20. For both negative and positive interpretations of the Marian tradition from a feminist perspective see: Elisabeth Moltmann-Wendel, "Motherhood or Friendship," in *Mary in the Churches* (Concilium Vol. 168), 17–22; Kari Børresen, "Mary in Catholic Theology," ibid. 48–56; Catharina Halkes, "Mary and Women," ibid. 66–73; Carol F. Jegen, ed., *Mary According to Women* (Kansas City, MO: Leaven Press, 1985); Elizabeth Johnson, "The Marian Tradition

and the Reality of Women," *Horizons* 12 (1985), 116–35; Patricia Noone, *Mary for Today* (Chicago: Thomas More Press, 1977); Rosemary Radford Ruether, *Mary: The Feminine Face of the Church* (Philadelphia: Westminster, 1977), and "Mariology as Symbolic Ecclesiology: Repression or Liberation?" in *Sexism and God-Talk* (Boston: Beacon Press, 1983), 139–58.

21. Paul VI, *Marialis Cultus* article 56, in *The Pope Speaks* 19 (1974–75), 84.

22. Metz, "Dogma as a Dangerous Memory," in *Faith in History and Society*, 200–04; Matthew Lamb, *Solidarity with Victims*, 107–15.

Gospel Portrait of Mary: Images and Symbols from the Synoptic Tradition

Donald Senior

A regeneration, perhaps even a revolution, in the church's devotion to Mary is taking place. One of the continuing catalysts for that regeneration is the church's closer attention to its biblical foundations. In mariology, as in every aspect of the church's life, attentive reading of the scriptures opens the way to new perspectives and helps us retrieve lost wisdom. The portrayal of Mary in the synoptic gospels contains some brushstrokes at times only dimly perceived by traditional mariology. Following a general survey of the data in these three gospels this paper will address some of the more unconventional aspects of Mary found in the synoptic gospels.

OVERVIEW OF THE SYNOPTIC MATERIAL

Traditional mariology has concentrated on Mary's identity as mother of God. This privileged link to Jesus Christ is the foundation on which the various attributes of Mary have been based and the fuel for most popular devotion to Mary through the ages. Mary's role as mother of Jesus is a fundamental datum of the New Testament and, ultimately, is the lynch pin for all other scriptural assertions about her. But, as more recent mariology has insisted, it would be a mistake to assume that Mary's motherhood commands the complete attention of the New Testament materials. In fact, a strong case can be made that the evangelists move their readers' attention away from Mary's blood ties to Jesus and focus much more tightly on bonds of discipleship and faith.[1]

<h2 style="text-align:center">MARY IN THE GOSPEL OF MARK</h2>

A review of the synoptic materials makes this clear. Mark's gospel gives scant attention to the mother of Jesus but already in Mark the trend of later gospel development is detectable. Mary is mentioned twice in Mark, neither time in particularly flattering circumstances. In 3:21 the "family" of Jesus stands outside a house in Capernaum where he is preaching; they are there to "seize" him and take him back home because of reports that he was "beside himself." Seemingly allied to the family, since they are mentioned in the same verse, are scribes "from Jerusalem" who accuse Jesus of being in league with Beelzebul (3:22). Later in 3:31–35 we learn that Mark includes in the "family" the "mother" and "brothers" of Jesus. When Jesus is notified of their presence he emphatically distances himself from his blood family; he gestures to the crowd sitting around him in the house listening to his preaching and declares: "Here are my mother and my brothers! Whoever does the will of God is my brother, and sister, and mother" (3:34–35). The gospel draws a sharp line between blood ties and discipleship ties and leaves no doubt that true kinship with Jesus is based on the latter.

This lesson is reinforced in the only other reference to Mary in Mark's gospel.[2] Jesus' return to his hometown of Nazareth ("his own country" as Mark refers to it, 6:1) is an unhappy one. His teaching in the synagogue and his reputation for performing "mighty works" "scandalize" the hometown crowd: "Where did this man get all this? What is the wisdom given to him? What mighty works are wrought by his hands! Is not this the carpenter, the son of Mary and brother of James and Joses and Judas and Simon, and are not his sisters here with us?" (6:2–3)

Much speculation has surrounded the phrase "son of Mary." Why not "son of Joseph"? Does this imply knowledge of the virginal conception on Mark's part? Or does it imply some slur on Jesus as illegitimate? Or does it simply mean that Joseph is dead and off the scene? Mark does not supply the answer to any of these questions. What is clear, however, is Mark's understanding of the overall scene. Those with the closest blood ties to Jesus—his family and his clan—reject him. So strong is their lack of faith that Jesus is "unable" to work miracles in Nazareth (6:5). This interpretation comes from the most authoritative character in the scene, Jesus himself: "A prophet is not without honor, except in his own country, and *among his own kin,* and in his own house" (6:4).

In the overall context of Mark's theology, these scenes have a clear message. Authentic kinship with Jesus is not based on blood ties. Only those who are called to discipleship and are willing to respond to that call are able to understand and accept Jesus as the very "gospel of God."

MARY IN THE GOSPELS OF MATTHEW AND LUKE

Matthew and Luke follow this lead of Mark but are unwilling to portray the mother of Jesus simply as a foil to authentic discipleship. In these gospels, particularly in Luke, Mary emerges not only as one with a unique blood tie to Jesus but as a model of discipleship.

In Luke's case, the fundamental principle is stated in Jesus' interpretation of the parable of the sower in chapter 8. The seed that falls on good soil represents those authentic disciples who, "hearing the word, hold it fast in an honest and good heart, and bring forth fruit with patience" (8:15). There is little doubt that this perspective guides Luke's portrayal of Mary. Mary is alluded to twice in the body of the gospel. In 11:27–28, an exuberant listener calls out to Jesus: "Blessed is the womb that bore you, and the breasts that you sucked!" But Jesus shunts direct praise for his mother in a different direction: "Blessed rather are those who hear the word of God and keep it!" Mary's ties to Jesus as mother are not rejected but the ties of discipleship are the more important source of blessing.

The same point is made in Luke's rendition of the Capernaum story. Unlike Mark's version (see Mk 3:21), the family's determination to come and retrieve Jesus is not mentioned at the beginning of the story. Nor does Luke drive a wedge between Jesus' blood family and his family of disciples in the scene that follows. After Jesus is told that his "mother and (his) brothers are standing outside, desiring to see you," he replies: "My mother and my brothers are those who hear the word of God and do it" (Lk 8:19–21). A direct reading of Luke's account does not exclude the mother of Jesus from being counted among those "who hear the word of God and do it."

The foundation of Luke's portrayal of Mary as model disciple is laid in the infancy narrative. Dramatic encounter with the word of God comes in the annunciation scene (1:26–37). Gabriel, a heavenly messenger sent from God, brings word that Mary is chosen to bear in her womb the "Son of the Most High," the one who will be given "the throne of his father David." Her child is destined to "reign over the house of Jacob forever" and his "kingdom shall have no end." Mary's response is encased in the typical literary form of biblical annunciation narratives with their usual exclamations of consternation and wonderment.[3] But her response is clear and exemplary from Luke's point of view: "Behold, I am the handmaid of the Lord; let it be to me according to your word" (1:37). Mary's credentials as hearer and doer of the word are impeccable.

The visitation scene that follows is further confirmation of this. Mary is lauded by Elizabeth for being the "mother of my Lord" (1:43) but also for being someone who "believed that there would be a fulfillment of what was spoken to her from the Lord" (1:45). This text, in fact, perfectly parallels the scene in the body of the gospel where the woman in the crowd praises Mary's physical motherhood, to be followed immediately by Jesus' praise for the one who hears the word and keeps it (Lk 11:27–28). Mary's pondering of the gospel events at the birth of Jesus (2:19) and at the beginning of his adulthood (2:51) are further signs of her discipleship: she continues to turn the meaning of the word over in her heart.

Luke closes his gospel portrayal with one final vignette about Mary the disciple. In Acts 1:14 "Mary, the mother of Jesus," is listed among those members of the Jerusalem community awaiting the storm of the Spirit at Pentecost. This had been the risen Christ's final charge to his disciples: "And behold, I send the promise of my Father upon you; but stay in the city, until you are clothed with power from on high" (Lk 24:49; see also Acts 1:4). Mary remains with the other disciples, awaiting the final redemptive act of the triumphant and ascendant Jesus who would send on that expectant community his promised Spirit.

As we shall see, the figure of Mary plays a small but significant role in Matthew, principally in the infancy narrative. But Matthew, too, softens Mark's negative portrayal of Mary in the body of the gospel. In the encounter at the house in Capernaum (Mt 12:46–50), Matthew, similar to Luke, omits the aggressive stance of the family coming to seize Jesus; they simply want to speak to him (Mt 12:46). And in the parallel to Mark 6 where Jesus returns to Nazareth, Matthew's version of Jesus' saying omits any reference to "his own kin." The saying now reads: "A prophet is not without honor except in his own country and in his own house." (Note that Luke's version of this saying in the similar but uniquely framed story of Jesus' inaugural preaching in the synagogue of Nazareth reads, "no prophet is acceptable in his own country"—4:24.)

While these scenes in Matthew hardly portray Mary as a disciple, they do reflect the more positive presentation of the mother of Jesus found in the infancy narrative. Unlike Luke, Matthew focuses on Joseph as the true hero of his story. But Mary, too, is presented in close solidarity with Jesus and, along with Joseph, is obedient to the divine will revealed through the medium of Joseph's dreams. As we shall see, Matthew's unique contribution to mariology may come in another somewhat neglected aspect of his infancy narrative.

This quick survey confirms one of the fundamental impulses of recent mariology. While Mary is clearly proclaimed as

the mother of Jesus, the synoptic evangelists are most concerned with her role as a follower of Jesus. Mark uses Mary,
along with the other family members of Jesus and, indeed, the
Jewish leaders and other characters in the narrative, as foils to
the true meaning of discipleship: that is, a bond with Jesus
founded on faith not on blood ties or status. Luke, and to a
lesser extent Matthew, are more insistent on this theme but use
Mary not as a foil to authentic discipleship but as positive expo-
nent of it. She is praised because she is an active hearer and
doer of God's word, thereby revealing that she has true kinship
with the Spirit of her son.

MARY AS UNCONVENTIONAL WOMAN

Neither motherhood nor discipleship in the terms described thus far exhaust the New Testament's portrayal of
Mary. Other aspects are also present, aspects that have been
emphasized in "third eye" theologies developed by some
Christian feminists and liberation theologians.

1. Mary as Scandal in the Gospel of Matthew

Mary's role in Matthew's gospel is confined almost exclusively to the infancy narrative. The most intriguing references
come in chapter 1, describing the circumstances of Jesus' conception (see Mt 1:18–25). All of Matthew's infancy narrative is
told from the perspective of Joseph, including these peculiar
verses.

Jewish marriage customs of the first century usually involved a two-step process: (1) the formal exchange of the cou-
ple's consent before witnesses (*'erusin*); this was legally binding
as a marriage but the bride continued to live with her family; (2)
the taking of the bride to the husband's home (*nisu'in*); from
this point on the husband was obliged to financially support his
wife. Matthew's account seems to reflect this situation. Between
the betrothal and the taking of Mary to Joseph's home, she is
found to be pregnant. Joseph is caught in a terrible dilemma.
The text describes him as "being a just man and unwilling to

put her to shame" and, therefore, resolving to divorce her quietly (1:19). The meaning of "just" here is not certain. Does it emphasize that Joseph is obedient to the law and therefore determined not to be betrothed to one who has committed adultery? Or, as seems more probable, is Joseph "just" because he chooses the more compassionate course of not exposing Mary to shame or punishment for her apparent infidelity but simply divorcing her quietly?

What is clear, and important for understanding Matthew's overall meaning, is that a shroud of scandal covers the circumstances of Jesus' conception. Only the message of an "angel of the Lord" who speaks to Joseph in a dream resolves the mystery: "Joseph, son of David, do not fear to take Mary your wife, for that which is conceived in her is of the Holy Spirit; she will bear a son, and you shall call his name Jesus, for he will save his people from their sins" (Mt 1:20–21). Matthew goes on to wrap the entire event in scriptural fulfillment: "All this took place to fulfill what the Lord had spoken by the prophet: 'Behold a virgin shall conceive and bear a son, and his name shall be called Emmanuel' (which means, God with us)" (Mt 1:22–23).

"All of this," Matthew states, "took place to fulfill what the Lord had spoken by the prophet." Presumably the "all" refers not simply to the conception of Jesus but also to the strange manner in which it took place.

That aura of the unusual and unexpected is highlighted in the genealogy with which Matthew introduces the vignette of Jesus' conception. Some authors, in fact, consider the verses dealing with the conception of Jesus to be a "footnote" or extension of the genealogy.[4] The genealogy is a hidden treasure in Matthew's gospel, masking major themes of his entire narrative in the seemingly innocuous drone of a genealogical form. As the summary verse reveals (1:17), the genealogy moves from Abraham to David to exile to the Messiah, whiplashing the reader from one end of Jewish history to the other. It moves from moments of humble beginnings to glorious apexes, from shattering tragedy to fulfillment of promise. The rhythm of the genealogy is steady as it counts off the patriarchal lines (this is particularly evident in the cadences of the Greek but is lost in most English translations): Abraham begot Isaac, Isaac begot Jacob, Jacob begot Judas and his brothers . . . and so on. Matthew in fact draws most of the content of this from the first book of Chronicles and the book of Ruth.[5]

But this soothing biological rhythm is taken out of syncopation on four occasions by references to women; the phrase Matthew appends in each case to introduce the woman, *ek tes,* ruptures the cadence of the generations and makes the reader take note. While a few women are mentioned in other biblical genealogies, never are they as frequent as in the brief genealogy of Matthew's gospel. Even more significant is the identity of these four: Tamar, a Canaanite, in Genesis 38:24 sits by the roadside playing the role of a prostitute in order to seduce her father-in-law Judah, because he had reneged on his promise to have one of his other sons carry out the obligations of the Levirate marriage in Tamar's behalf. Rahab, a Canaanite prostitute of Jericho, shelters in her home the Israelite spies who reconnoiter the land before the great battle for its possession (Jos 2). Ruth, a Moabite, with the aid of Naomi, secures Boaz as her husband after approaching him at night on the threshing floor. Bathsheba, a Hittite (but identified by Matthew as "the wife of Uriah"), is the object of David's lust, and to procure her for himself he is willing to commit adultery and murder (2 Sam 11); later she would become the mother of Solomon.

Interpreters of Matthew's gospel have been divided over the reason why the evangelist introduces such women into the family tree of Jesus. At least three major theories have been suggested:[6] (1) All of the women are sinners; Matthew may introduce them to forecast the fact that Jesus will save his people from their sins. But later Jewish tradition considered Rahab and Ruth as heroines, and it is not clear that Matthew or Jewish tradition in general considered these women as notorious sinners. (2) All of them are foreigners; Matthew thereby introduces his theme of the Gentile mission. However Matthew does not seem to emphasize their non-Israelite origin in his genealogy, and this does not offer a promising link to Mary who is clearly Jewish and is the fifth woman of the genealogy. (3) The four women share irregular marriage unions yet were

vehicles of God's messianic plan. Matthew's theology emphasizes that God works through the extraordinary and the unexpected. God's initiative is not dependent on human continuity
and decorum.

This third theory seems the most promising, but a recent
and bold feminist interpretation of this text pushes it a bit
further. In her book *The Illegitimacy of Jesus,* Jane Schaberg sees
this text as a key to a startling historical fact that stands behind
the infancy narratives of both Matthew and Luke, namely that
Jesus was illegitimately conceived, either through seduction or
rape (she considers the latter the most likely).[7] While this hypothesis may sound quite radical and sensational, it is, in fact, a
very ancient speculation and one that Schaberg poses in a serious and respectful manner.

Her major arguments are drawn from Matthew: (1) The
presence of the four women prepares for an illegitimate conception in which God does not interfere. (2) The passive verb
eqennethe ("was begotten of Mary") in Matthew 1:16 should not
be interpreted as a so-called "divine passive" but as a veiled
reference to the human and illegitimate conception of Jesus. (3)
The puzzling omission of one generation in the last section of
the genealogy (where Matthew cites fourteen but only thirteen
are present) is another veiled reference to the absent biological
father of Jesus. (4) In the quote from Isaiah 7:14 ("behold a
'virgin' shall conceive and bear a son . . .") *parthenos* should be
translated as "young woman" and not "virgin" to reflect the
original Hebrew sense.

Therefore, according to Schaberg, Matthew veils but does
not entirely remove the evidence of Jesus' illegitimacy. Even
though his viewpoint is predominantly male and is expressed
through Joseph's dominant role in the narrative, still a radical
biblical theology centering around Mary and the other women
of the genealogy emerges. God does not simply work in extraordinary circumstances, nor does God simply bring continuity
where humans see only discontinuity. Both are important but
incomplete insights of more traditional exegesis of these texts.
Jesus' illegitimacy illustrates a "divine accommodation to
human freedom in the complexity of near tragedy"—a story

which the genealogy shows is "without precedent but not without preparation" in the biblical history.[8] The action of God does not replace human freedom or human paternity but works in and through it. "God," says Schaberg, "is one who sides with the outcast, the endangered woman and her child."[9]

Schaberg's thesis about the human paternity of Jesus seems to run directly counter to traditional Roman Catholic theology of the virginal conception. But it suffers from more than doctrinal difficulties. Its major difficulty is that it pits Matthew against Matthew. Through his narrator, the evangelist gives the fundamental interpretation of the scene: "that which is conceived in her is of the Holy Spirit" (1:20). The whisper of scandal is present in Matthew's story not because it is a vestige of historical tradition unsuccessfully camouflaged by the evangelist but because it provides a human foil to the divine revelation which Joseph (and, through him, the reader) receives in his dream. If Matthew were at the same time asserting, even in a veiled fashion, that Jesus was conceived by human paternity, illegitimate or not, his entire narrative loses its coherence. The passive verb in 1:16 must be a divine passive because it is to cohere with what the gospel will tell the reader in 1:20 (the conception of Jesus is through the power of God's Spirit). The fulfillment formula of 1:23 reads *parthenos* or "virgin" because that is precisely Matthew's point in the preceding section. The absent generation in the third part of the genealogy, whatever its explanation (and there are several plausible ones), cannot stand on its own as an argument for an omitted human father in a narrative which explicitly states otherwise.

But if Schaberg's speculation about the historical traditions behind the infancy narrative of Matthew is unconvincing, her theological reflections on the meaning of Matthew's text are more successful. Reaction to her main thesis about the historical illegitimacy of Jesus should not cloud the powerful biblical theology it contains. The physical illegitimacy of Jesus is not essential to support a theology that proclaims that the God of Israel and the God of Jesus sides with the outcast, the endangered woman and her child. Matthew proclaims that quite clearly in the cases of the women of the genealogy. Through them God works in history: through the abused Tamar who suffers injustice from Judah and his sons; through Rahab, a Canaanite prostitute who becomes a heroine of Jewish liberation; through Ruth, vulnerable Moabite who enters the messianic line; through Bathsheba who is violated by the king, whose husband is murdered, whose life is appropriated to the royal purposes without negotiation or discussion, and yet who becomes a vital link in the Davidic history.

The same is true of Mary. She is not a member of the Davidic line but becomes so only through Joseph's espousal of her; she is "illegitimate" royalty (as is Jesus!). She is vulnerable to the sanctions of the law and liable to rigorous punishment. She is voiceless in Matthew's narrative. Yet she, along with her extraordinary predecessors, becomes the arena of sacred history and the locus where the divine promises to Israel are fulfilled. This distaff biblical theology in which "illegitimate," apparently insignificant, seemingly defenseless, yet startlingly powerful people become the agents of God's action in history is carried through in the rest of the infancy narrative and, indeed, in the rest of Matthew's gospel. A mix of tragedy and grace follows the family of Jesus as they experience threat, exile, and displacement. Jesus the Bethlehemite must live as a refugee in Nazareth; because of King Archelaus' cruelty, the family cannot return home. In this strange way, God's liberating gospel will be proclaimed first in Galilee, the place Matthew calls the Galilee of the Gentiles, where the people sit listlessly in darkness and the shadow of death awaiting the moment of liberation as God had promised (see Mt 4:12–17).

A stream of characters will flow through the gospel of Matthew, many of them unusual, foreign, and illegitimate from the perspective of Israel's history and the strictures of the law. But each is capable of responding to and exemplifying the gospel in a vivid way: the Gentile magi who recognize the Messiah despite the treachery of Herod and his Jerusalem court, the leper, the paralytic, the feverish mother-in-law of Peter, the Gentile demoniac of Gadarene, the hemorrhaging woman and vast crowds of other sick and disabled people who cross the boundaries to touch Jesus and vigorously believe in him, the

Canaanite woman who will not take no for an answer, the Roman centurion whose faith shakes even Jesus and gives him a vision of a new family of Abraham coming from east and west, the tax collector Matthew and his socially repugnant friends who join Jesus' mission. These and other characters in the gospel amplify the message first embodied in Mary and the women of the genealogy. The God of Israel, the God revealed in Jesus, sides with the outcast, the endangered, the tabooed, the illegitimate.

The most radical illustration of this theological principle is Jesus himself: born of a non-Davidic woman, yet messianic king; called to heal and save God's people, yet himself struck down and crucified; sent to Israel, yet rejected by its teachers and leaders; broken in death, yet risen triumphant and ever present with his church.

There is little doubt that Matthew highlights this theme for the benefit of his own mixed community of Jewish and Gentile Christians. It was a time of critical transition when part of the community resisted change and hurled accusations of illegitimacy and impropriety toward Gentiles seeking entry in the community. Matthew tells the story of Jesus whose God-driven life is rooted in the unexpected and the inappropriate—whose origins and mission shattered well-sealed boundaries and illuminated the presence of grace in people and situations branded sinful. The mariology of Matthew's Gospel is in fact identical to its christology.

2. Mary as Promise Unfulfilled in Luke's Gospel

Luke, too, presents Mary in unconventional tones quite different from the themes of discipleship and messianic motherhood that dominate traditional interpretation of this gospel. Here, too, the approach of liberation theology that reads the texts from the distaff side, from the vantage point of the oppressed, helps alert us to deeper dimensions of Luke's narrative.

One of the most intriguing scenes in Luke's infancy gospel is the visitation (1:39–56). This scene seems to escape most of the attempts to find a smooth parallel structure in the overall infancy gospel of Luke.[10] It is the only scene in the entire gospel literature where two women meet and hold center stage.

More significant for Luke's mariology, this is the scene that ties together the two parallel conception stories of John the Baptist and Jesus which provide the substratum for Luke's entire infancy narrative. Within the dynamics of Luke's story, the scene brings together two main protagonists, Elizabeth, mother-to-be of the last and greatest prophet John, and Mary, mother-to-be of the messiah Jesus. As most commentators point out, Luke reaffirms in this scene the superiority of Jesus to John, a leitmotif of the entire infancy narrative.

But something more is going on. It is interesting to ask, simply on the level of the narrative Luke provides, what binds these two women together. They are kinswomen (1:36), so the younger woman Mary comes to visit with her older relative during her pregnancy. Another important bond is that both are expecting children, a point emphasized in that the child within the womb of Elizabeth leaps for joy at the approach of the child in the womb of Mary (and thereby the superiority of Jesus is proclaimed).

However, Luke has tied these women together in another, perhaps more subtle way. Both women are caught up in an extraordinary way in the fulfillment theology of Luke's gospel. Luke portrays Elizabeth as another Sarah, righteous yet barren; and now the old age of Zachary and his wife has made barrenness seem a permanent curse (1:7). Luke evokes a recurrent biblical motif, the tragedy and lament of barrenness overcome only through the lavish, rejuvenating power of God who brings life to the empty womb.[11]

Mary, too, is linked to the Lukan theme of promise unexpectedly fulfilled. In Mary's case, the problem is not old age but virginity: "How shall this be, since I have no husband?" she tells the angel (1:34). Traditional mariology has presumed that the virginity of Mary is presented in Luke's text as treasured virtue. But there is reason to suggest that Luke considers it an impoverishment, a promise unfulfilled and with no prospect in sight. Luke explicitly links the plight of Elizabeth—no birth because of old age, clearly a tragic situation in biblical culture—with Mary's virginity. In responding to Mary's protest of impossibility ("I have no husband"), the angel recalls the parallel situation of Elizabeth: "And behold, your kinswoman Elizabeth in her old age has also conceived a son; and this is the sixth month with her who was called barren. For with God nothing will be impossible" (1:36–37). The implication is clear: no matter how tragic or impoverished the situation, barrenness or virginity, God can do the impossible.

This interpretation is reinforced by other aspects of the visitation scene. In addition to praising Mary for her motherhood (as does the voice from the crowd in Luke 11:27), Elizabeth cites Mary's trust "that there would be a fulfillment of what was spoken to her from the Lord" (1:45). Despite the emptiness of her virginity and the fact of her having no husband, Mary believes that God can bring life into her womb.

Mary's canticle, sung at her meeting with Elizabeth, is another important element. The Magnificat draws much of its inspiration from the canticle of Hannah in 1 Samuel 2:1–10. Hannah, the wife of Elkanah, was unable to bear children. Peninnah, the second wife of Elkanah, was fertile and gave her husband many sons and daughters. This pleased Elkanah and he used to give the choice portions at table to Peninnah, who would ridicule Hannah for her infertility.

Hannah pleaded with God for deliverance: "O Lord of hosts, if thou wilt indeed look on the affliction of thy maidservant, and remember me, and not forget thy maidservant, but wilt give to thy maidservant a son, then I will give him to the Lord all the days of his life, and no razor shall touch his head" (1 Sam 1:11). That wrenching plea is finally heard when the priest Eli sees Hannah praying through her tears at the shrine of Shiloh and promises that God will hear her prayer. At the joy of new life in her womb, Hannah breaks out into her canticle of deliverance, a hymn that praises the God who shatters the bows of the mighty but "gives seven children to the barren" (1 Sam 2:1–10).

Mary's Magnificat echoes many of the basic themes and phrases of Hannah's canticle. It, too, is a prayer of praise for

God's fidelity to the weak and the poor, the God who "has regarded the low estate of his handmaiden," who puts down the mighty from their thrones and exalts those of low degree, who fills the hungry with good things and sends the rich away empty. The "low estate" of Mary in Luke's narrative is her virginity. She is destined to bear the messiah but she has no husband. Into the poverty of her virginity, God brings new and unexpected life.

Thus both Elizabeth and Mary exemplify two different experiences of promises unfulfilled. For Elizabeth it is the experience of opportunity lost. The passage of time and the specter of death have stillborned her hopes for bearing life. For Mary (similar to Hannah, who is not branded as "old") the experience is one of having hopes for the future without expectation that fulfillment of them is possible. The related and tragic experiences of regret and frustration are exemplified in the barrenness of each of these women of the infancy gospel.

Thus Luke presents Mary as one of the lowly—as an Israelite who has experienced the poverty of unfulfilled hopes, of promises destined not to be made true. But the God of Jesus breaks into this barrenness and fulfills the promise, bringing new life where it was judged impossible by every human standard.

One does not need to go far in Luke's gospel to learn that "fulfillment" is a major theological category. From start to finish, Luke frames the gospel drama in the language of promise fulfilled. In the inaugural scene at Nazareth (4:21) Jesus proclaims that he and his liberating mission embody the fulfillment of God's promises to Israel. And the gospel will close with the risen Christ declaring that he will send "the promise of my Father upon you" in the form of the Spirit (24:49). The God of Luke's gospel is the faithful God who remembers the promises made to Israel, promises of liberating redemption especially for the lowly. Mary, therefore, exemplifies this theology and christology.

Using the theme of barrenness does seem to cast Mary (as well as Elizabeth) in a passive mode, as was true with Matthew's portrayal. Some feminist interpreters would point out that the evangelists and their traditions are still trapped in the mechanics of male sexuality, with the women dependent on the vital impulse from a patriarchal God.

While this objection has some validity, it might be questioned whether Luke intends to portray Mary (or Elizabeth) as purely passive or as passive because they are women. From the biblical perspective, everyone—male and female—is, in a certain sense, passive before the power of God. But this is not cast as a servile or flaccid passivity. It is a stance of trust in God's loving power and life-sustaining fidelity, an active expectation that God is faithful. The hearer of the word, in Luke's theology, must also be the doer of the word. And Mary—in her emphatic yes, in her active pondering of the word, in her visit to her kinswoman, in her strong and prophetic canticle, in her presence with the post-Easter community—is portrayed as acting on the word.

The importance of Mary's child-bearing should not be forgotten in the attention to other symbols and themes of the gospel. All of the great biblical characters who experience release from barrenness bear great children for God, bringing into being through humanity's most startlingly creative act—birthing—the fulfillment of God's promise to Israel. Luke calls Mary the "mother of (the) Lord," a powerful, royal title. At the most fundamental level of Luke's story, Mary, through her exceedingly creative act of giving birth to Jesus, is the one who enables the life of Israel to be redeemed.

Thus both Matthew and Luke portray Mary in unconventional terms: Mary as scandalous woman with whom God identifies; Mary as vessel of poverty whom God enriches; Mary judged powerless yet crafting history's most explosive transformation. These same prophetic dynamics of reversal are applied to Jesus in the gospels and become the bedrock of their paschal mystery.

In a world racked with injustice, where the lament of promises never fulfilled and the frustration of hopes doomed to despair are the bitter bread of millions, the unconventional dimensions of the gospel portrayals of Mary seem to have more substance and appeal than ever before. Neither of these motifs allows the mother of Jesus to be put on a patriarchal pedestal or to be iconized out of our experience. The battered woman, the single parent without resources, the displaced family, the young who live with despair, the old who are discarded—these are the children of God addressed in the distaff side of gospel mariology. From such biblical roots can come new and powerful impulses for the church's spirituality.

Notes

1. See the general surveys provided in A. Tambasco, *What Are They Saying About Mary?* (New York: Paulist, 1984), and R. Brown, K. Donfried, J. Fitzmyer, J. Reuman (eds.), *Mary in the New Testament* (Philadelphia: Fortress, 1978).
2. The reference to "Mary, the mother of James" in Mark 15:40, 47, 61 cannot be to Mary the mother of Jesus.
3. See, further, R. Brown, *The Birth of the Messiah* (Garden City, NY: Doubleday, 1977), 292–98.
4. See K. Stendahl, " 'Quis et Unde?' An analysis of Mt 1–2," in W. Eltester (ed.), *Judentum, Urchristentum, Kirche* (Festschrift J. Jeremias; BZNW 26; Berlin: Töpelmann, 1964), 94–105.
5. Compare 1 Chr 2:10–15; Ru 4:18–22.
6. See R. Brown et al. (eds.), *Mary in the New Testament*, 77–83.
7. Jane Schaberg, *The Illegitimacy of Jesus: A Feminist Theological Interpretation of the Infancy Narratives* (San Francisco: Harper & Row, 1987).
8. Ibid. p. 34.
9. Ibid. p. 74.
10. See R. Brown, *The Birth of the Messiah*, 339–41.
11. See Mary Callaway, *Sing, O Barren One*. A Study in Comparative Midrash (Dissertation Series 91) Atlanta: Scholars Press, 1986; esp. pp. 100–107.

ᗰary in
Johannine Ꮯraditions

Pheme Perkins

PERSON OR SYMBOL? THE MARIAN DILEMMA

Twentieth century biblical interpretation has often focused on using tools of cultural, historical, and archaeological analysis to recover the historical setting of persons and events mentioned in the Bible. People desire some insight into what it might have meant for an actual human person to live out faith in the God of scripture in a "world" that becomes more meaningful to us as its details become more concrete. Sometimes the attempt to apply this approach to "Mary" leads to speculation about the possibility of a human paternity of Jesus—even, most recently, of Mary as rape victim (a charge not unknown in antiquity).[1] The difficulty with any such "quest of the historical Mary" is that we possess very little historical information from which to construct a picture.[2]

People often look to such historicizing images of Mary as a way of overcoming the distance between Mary and contemporary experience that has been created by the elaborate symbolisms of Marian piety. Theologians seeking a more ecumenical approach to "mariology" hope that emphasis upon historical reconstruction and biblical data can demonstrate that Mary is indeed "mother of all Christians." Such approaches may begin to overcome the gulf between Catholics and Protestants that was opened up by the definition of such Marian dogmas as the immaculate conception and the assumption. As Fr. Raymond Brown has already pointed out, dogmas of this sort are not directly derived from New Testament evidence. The most that the Catholic exegete can do is argue that they are not contradictory to what the New Testament does affirm or suggest about Mary.[3]

It is not my primary task to assess such later theological developments. However, the images of Mary which we find in "Johannine writings"[4] do have a bearing upon the evolution of much Marian doctrine. "Mary" in the New Testament is already perceived in symbolic, not personal, terms. She is already so completely subsumed into an author's symbolic understanding of the significance of Jesus and his ministry that the question of the "historical" Mary cannot be appropriately applied. The authors of the fourth gospel and of the book of Revelation are quite clear on this point. Perhaps no one would dispute that the image of the "woman clothed with the sun" in Revelation 12, which tradition associated with Mary, is symbolic. Indeed, the exegetical issue is often posed in terms of whether or not "Mary" is the intended referent of the symbol.[5]

The gospel is no less "symbolic" in its presentation. However, readers are often taken in by the literary style of "realistic narrative" and presume that historical events and interactions are to be recovered from the two episodes which mention the "mother" of Jesus, the wedding at Cana (Jn 2:1–12) and the scene with the beloved disciple at the foot of the cross (Jn 19:26–27). A few rather simple observations are sufficient to indicate why such a presupposition would seriously bias the approach to the text. John always refers to the woman in question as "his mother," even in 19:25. There the evangelist gives us names of other "Marys" associated with Jesus and known to us from synoptic traditions as well as the peculiar notice that Jesus' mother had a sister, Mary, the mother of Clopas.[6] While John 19:25 parallels the other gospels and refers to women who had accompanied Jesus and were present at the crucifixion, vv. 26–27 suddenly speak of Mary as if she were standing alone with the beloved disciple. The latter is also never named and clearly functions as a symbolic figure throughout the events of

Jesus' final instructions to his disciples, his crucifixion, and his resurrection. Though he appears to have been an historical follower of Jesus and is said to be the "witness" behind its tradition (Jn 21:24), we have no clues about him as an historical personage.

The evangelist's presentation of the miracle at Cana associates Jesus' mother with his "hour" through the refusal to perform the "sign" because the hour had not yet come (Jn 2:4). Yet, as so often happens when John is editing traditional material,[7] this comment has no apparent impact on the story which proceeds as a "gift" miracle.[8] Evidently the association between the two scenes has been established by the author. The interpreter must attempt to discover what the significance of these two scenes might have been for readers in the Johannine community.

Mary's role is established by these two cryptic scenes. Either the fourth gospel does not know traditions about Jesus' conception, birth, and ties to Bethlehem, or these traditions are ignored. One might have expected some hint of such a tradition in the allusions to Jesus' "origins" which figure prominently in John (e.g. Jn 7:40–43). However, for the fourth gospel, Jesus' origins are always heavenly, "from the Father," and as such contrast with the earthly origins of those whom he confronts (e.g. Jn 8:23). This symbolism renders the question of Jesus' human origins irrelevant.

JESUS' MOTHER AT CANA (JN 2:1–12)

Jesus' mother first appears in a miracle story where she instigates the miraculous gift of wine by first commenting on the lack of wine and then providing instructions for the servants. The verses which frame this episode (vv. 1, 12) suggest that she was already associated with Jesus and his disciples.[9] Since the disciples have been pictured in the previous verses (1:35–51) as persons with correct but insufficient (v. 51) understanding of Jesus' messianic identity, the reader should assume that Mary's actions in this story follow a similar pattern.[10] Though v. 11 may have been formulated on the basis of a "signs source" which understood Jesus' miracles as evidence of his divine identity,[11] the evangelist probably linked the reference to manifestation of Jesus' glory and the disciples' belief in Jesus with the conclusion to the previous episode (vv. 50–51). There an affirmation of faith based on Jesus' mysterious knowledge of Nathanael is questioned by allusion to the coming manifestation of Jesus as heavenly Son of Man.

Similarly, this story twice places in question the faith engendered by the "sign" Jesus will do. First is Jesus' apparent refusal to respond to his mother's request since it is not "his hour," that is, the real manifestation of Jesus' glory (e.g. Jn 3:14–15; 8:28; 12:23; 17:24).[12] Second is the rejection of a false faith based on "signs" which Jesus had done (2:23–25). A similar literary pattern can be traced in the raising of Lazarus (Jn 11:1–44). Jesus' apparent failure to act belongs to the "plot" set out by the evangelist at the introduction: this death will serve to glorify the Son of God (v. 4). Martha's initial confession of faith in the resurrection must be "corrected" by the appearance of Jesus as the resurrection and life (vv. 21–27). The miracle itself only occurs after that central insight has been achieved. Ironically, it serves to increase opposition to Jesus (and even to Lazarus; 12:9–11).

M.-E. Boismard detects a shift in the relationship between faith and miracles at two different stages in the evolution of the Johannine material. At one early stage, miracles were used for their apologetic value. They led to faith in Jesus as the "prophet like Moses." At a somewhat later stage, the relationship is reversed. Faith is prior to any miracle. Without faith in Jesus, the miracle is not even rightly understood.[13] What motivates such faith is the word of Jesus itself. All other forms of testimony are insufficient, since they cannot grasp the reality of Jesus' appearance in the world as the incarnate Word of God. In response to the question of whether or not the twelve will abandon Jesus along with others who have been scandalized by his words, Peter says, "Lord, to whom would we go? You have the words of eternal life" (6:68). This epitomizes the Johannine concept of faith.[14]

The evangelist has described Mary's response to Jesus in

such a way that her faith is never in doubt. She knows what he will do without having witnessed any miraculous signs. Some exegetes have also noticed the christological emphasis in the mysterious origin of the wine: "the steward tasted the water now become wine, and did not know where it came from" (v. 9). The question of "where" Jesus comes from will be persistently raised by those who reject his word as the one sent from God (e.g., 5:33–34; 6:32–51).[15] Indeed, the crowd's perception of the earthly origins of Jesus blocks their ability to recognize that he is the "bread from heaven which brings eternal life" (6:42).

John emphasizes the fact that those who respond to Jesus' word with faith must be drawn to him by God (6:43–45). Mary's role in the wedding at Cana is not direct evidence for Marian intercessory power as older exegetes held. Nor, as some radical moderns have proposed, is it evidence that she is excluded from the circle of believers. Instead it demonstrates that her relationship to Jesus is based on a true intuition of faith, not merely upon her biological relationship to him.[16]

MARY AS "MOTHER OF BELIEVERS" (JN 19:26–27)

The miracle at Cana set the stage for the evangelist's presentation of Mary at the "hour" of Jesus' glorification. We have seen that the evangelist redacted the traditional image of Mary as one of the women from Galilee who witnessed Jesus' death in order to create a special scene in which she and the beloved disciple are the object of Jesus' final instructions. This scene represents the apex of the cycle of scenes which begin with the elevation of Jesus on the cross and end with the removal of the body (Jn 19:16b–42). Throughout, John emphasizes the royal dignity of Jesus and the control which Jesus maintains over his own destiny. Jesus carries his own cross. He secures the future of those closest to him. He dies of his own accord, offering up his Spirit to the Father.[17]

This scene clearly refers the reader back to the opening scene at Cana. In the Johannine passion narrative this is the only place where the word "hour" occurs, and it is the second appearance of the mother of Jesus. The beloved disciple will be depicted as the epitome of faith which understands without need for confirming testimony. Therefore the relationship between Mary and this disciple must represent the community of true believers which it is Jesus' mission to establish (e.g., Jn 17:11–19). The inherited passion material might suggest that Jesus dies abandoned by his disciples and scorned by the crowd. The evangelist corrects this impression in two ways. Jesus' prediction of the flight of the disciples includes the affirmation that Jesus is never alone, never without the Father (16:32). Second, the nucleus of the believing community has not abandoned Jesus but is established at the foot of the cross.[18]

This passage has not yet developed the symbolism of Mary as mother of the church that would emerge from twelfth century Marian piety.[19] For Johannine Christians, the beloved disciple was the source of their tradition and the true interpreter of the meaning of what had happened in Jesus. His special relation to Jesus is evident in the Johannine supper scene where he reclines alongside Jesus and is the one to whom Peter addresses the question about who the betrayer will be (13:23–25). Mary's position is equivalent to that of this favored disciple, not yet elevated above it. Together they represent the successful culmination of Jesus' ministry since they have perceived his "glory" and testimony to the Father.

THE "GREAT SIGN" OF THE WOMAN CLOTHED WITH THE SUN (REVELATION 12)

When the fourth gospel's understanding of Jesus as incarnate Word is combined with the infancy narrative traditions of the synoptics, one has the foundation for the later understanding of Mary as "mother of God." Mary's heavenly exaltation as "mother of the faithful" requires the mythic imagery of Revelation 12 for its later development.[20] However, the imagery of the goddess mother of a divine child under attack by the dragon, the embodiment of evil, stems from much more archaic levels of mythology.[21] The imagery of Revelation 12 cannot be traced to any one rendering of the story, though it appears closest to that of Leto and Apollo. However, the opening image of the woman clothed with the sun would most naturally remind readers of the iconography of such goddesses as Ephesian Artemis, Syrian Atargatis, and the Egyptian Isis.

Adela Collins proposes a complex history of tradition for this chapter of Revelation. The imagery was, she suggests, originally employed in Hellenistic Jewish circles. The expulsion from heaven was linked to the story of the fallen angels. At the same time, a Jewish audience was familiar with imagery of Yahweh as the divine warrior coming to defeat the evil embodied in those political powers which oppress Israel. The "messianic" and political overtones of the passage would be clear enough. God's "messiah" is already waiting in heaven to lead the people out of oppression to a new era of cosmic peace and fertility.[22]

In an apocalyptic Jewish context the "woman" represents the heavenly embodiment of Israel. Adaptation of this imagery to the Christian understanding of Jesus as messiah introduces some incongruities in the storyline. The defeat of Satan as a prelude to new creation is an established apocalyptic motif (e.g. *T. Levi* 18, 10–12; *Ass. Mos.* 10, 1). Here that defeat has begun but has not yet been completed, since the community, the woman's offspring on earth, still awaits salvation. The chapter's Christian editor has reassured the community by inserting a "victory song" into the account in vv. 10–12.[23] The Satan figure in the heavens refers to the "accuser" in the heavenly court. Since he has been expelled from the heavens, faithful Christians do not have to fear that they will be accused before God. Thus the author has also shifted the "political" message of the imagery from nationalist apocalyptic to a theology of martyrdom. The faithful Christians may suffer persecution and even death for confessing Christ in the human courts. But that only embodies the dragon's attempt to attack those who belong to God. The martyr's death will be vindicated in God's judgment.[24]

The mythic symbolism of Revelation 12 is essential to later mariological developments. Mary takes on divine and cosmological attributes. However, in Revelation the explicit connection to the mother of Jesus has not been made. The "woman clothed with the sun" remains entirely within the realm of a mythic story whose intent is to reassure Christian martyrs.[25] They are invited to enact what is an essentially masculine archetype of the divine-child/hero through passive suffering rather than active resistance.[26] Christians must understand the persecution they experience as a reflection of the primordial hostility between the dragon and the woman and her divine son. Christian faith in this story represents the faithfulness of the martyr (vv. 10–12, 17b).

SECOND CENTURY DEVELOPMENTS

The stories of Mary linked to the ministry of Jesus are of no interest to second and third century authors. Their primary interest lies in the "virgin birth" of Jesus. Jesus' dual parentage reflects the coming together of divine and human.[27] One tradition even spoke of the Holy Spirit as "mother" of Jesus.[28] The *Ascension of Isaiah* expands on the Matthean accounts of Jesus' birth and virginal conception to show that for Jesus' mother the curse of Eve was lifted. The child emerges from the womb magically without the pangs of labor:

> And it came to pass, while they were alone that Mary straightway beheld with her eyes and saw a small child and she was amazed. And when the amazement wore off, her womb was found as it was before she was with child (*Asc. Is.* viii, 8–9).

The first extensive development of the parallelism between Mary and Eve appears in Justin Martyr (*Dial* 100). Her obedience reverses the disobedience of Eve, just as Christ serves as the new Adam in the divine plan of salvation. Justin also attributes the incarnation of the pre-existent Son to the activity of the divine Word. The thematic development of parallels between Mary and Eve serves to demonstrate the appropriate "divine economy" of salvation in Irenaeus. Since Satan gained power over man through a woman, it is appropriate that Satan be defeated by a woman (e.g. *Adv. Haer.* V f21, 1; III 21, 10; 24,

4).[29] Irenaeus' understanding of salvation as "recapitulation" leads to the image of Mary as mother of a new humanity.[30]

The astral themes associated with the woman in Revelation 12 reappear in the context of Jesus' incarnation as a descent into the world which "disturbs" the order of the astral deities. Ignatius of Antioch (*Ephesians* 19, 1–3) speaks of three mysteries which have eluded the ruler of this age: Mary's virginity, her giving birth, and the death of the Lord. The incarnation represents the destruction of all magic and the powers of death. Consequently the astral powers were disturbed. Several gnostic writings also link the descent of the heavenly revealer to cosmic destruction of the powers which govern this world and hold humans in bondage.[31] Destruction of the fates, the fallen angels, and the shaking of the stars all belong to the same symbolic context.[32] However, Mary does not figure in this context. Orthodox Christian writers understood the virgin birth to be an indication of Jesus' humanity. Gnostics might use the theme of "virgin" mother to indicate that the body used by the heavenly revealer was uncontaminated by passion (e.g. *2 Apoc. Jas.* CG V 51, 25–52, 1). But the docetic orientation of most gnostic christology makes it impossible to associate the descent of the divine revealer with the contamination of human embodiment.[33]

Ignatius of Antioch counters his docetic opponents by insisting that the "come in the flesh" of John 1:14 implies Jesus' true humanity. He insists that Christ has two natures, one human and one divine (e.g. *Smyr* 1, 1; *Tral* 9, 1). Whenever Ignatius speaks of Jesus' birth "from Mary," he is thinking of Jesus' true humanity rather than his divine origin (e.g. *Ephesians* 18, 2; 19, 1).[34] The quasi-credal phrasing of *Ephesians* 18, 2 includes a further reference to the suffering of Jesus "purifying the water." Some scholars have suggested that this tradition developed out of the mythic symbolism of the dragon fight.[35] A gnostic text (*Para. Shem* CG VII 37, 14–38, 6; 45, 20–23) rejects baptism in ordinary water because it is "demon-filled." Cyril of Jerusalem (*Catech.* 3:11) speaks of Christ descending into the water so that we can receive the power to tread on the head of the dragon. Syriac baptismal rites also celebrate this theme.

These examples of mythic recovery of the themes of the dragon battle and the casting out of the evil angels depart from the earlier example in Revelation in one important aspect: they do not develop the theme of the "goddess mother" and her divine child. The divinity of Christ is clearly tied with his heavenly origins as Word or revealer figure. Insofar as Mary appears, she is the one who provides the link between Jesus and humanity. As Irenaeus would argue, God used Mary rather than creating a body for the "new Adam" out of earth so that the "likeness" of the Adam being redeemed by Christ would be preserved (*Adv. Haer.* III 21, 10).

A WEALTH OF SYMBOLS: THE MARIAN DILEMMA

This brief exploration into Johannine traditions suggests that the dilemma of how to understand Mary's significance can hardly be resolved by appeal to the New Testament and early patristic period. She has already become a symbolic figure whose meaning is elaborated very differently in different contexts. The fourth gospel focuses upon Jesus' unique revelation of the Father. Only Jesus as one come "from heaven" speaks with God's authority and makes eternal life possible for those who believe. In this context Mary provides one image of the true believer. It is her faith, a faith shared by other figures like the beloved disciple, and not her biological relationship to Jesus which secures her special place in the gospel. Yet when the incarnation traditions of John are combined with the infancy narrative traditions, Mary's biological relationship to Jesus comes to the fore. She is the source of Jesus' humanity.

The mythic exploration of Revelation 12 is not initially linked to Mary at all. The myth concerns the goddess mother and divine child. Historically relating the myth to the peculiar Christian experiences of Satan's defeat, begun but not completed, opens the way for the emergence of Mary as "queen of heaven." However, Revelation seems to have addressed the mythic story to Christian martyrs who must meet the attacks of the beast. The seer affirms their vindication before God's judgment seat. All faithful martyrs share the fate imaged in the mythic story. To that extent the woman is their mother as well as mother of the Messiah. However, elements of this mythic pattern can recur without any reference to the story of the woman and child. The destruction of the fallen angels and their astral domination over the world seems to have been a more significant rendering of "incarnation as descent" traditions than the myth of the woman and child.

This brief exploration of the Johannine and second century traditions about Mary confronts us with the symbolic realities of religious discourse. "Mary" is a vehicle by which early Christians express insights about such realities as the nature of faith, the triumph of the believing community, the true humanity of the divine Son, and the reversal of Eve's "fall" in a new humanity made possible by the incarnation. At this stage of development Marian symbolism is not a speculative goal in itself. Rather its orientation is always to express or, in the antidocetic controversies about incarnation, to safeguard primary intuitions about christology and soteriology. At the same time, the diverse directions already opened up by these developments, such as the possibility of enthroning Mary as "queen of heaven" and mother of all believers, show that later developments of Marian symbolism can claim some roots in our earliest Christian heritage.

Notes

1. See J. Schaberg, *The Illegitimacy of Jesus* (San Francisco: Harper & Row, 1988).
2. See the general survey of data in R. Brown, K. Donfried, J. Fitzmyer and J. Reumann, eds., *Mary in the New Testament* (New York: Paulist/Philadelphia: Fortress, 1978).
3. See R. Brown, *Biblical Exegesis and Church Doctrine* (Mahwah: Paulist, 1985), 96–100.
4. This phrase refers to writings that antiquity attributed to "John," specifically the fourth gospel and the book of Rev-

elation, though the weight of the evidence suggests that the only direct connection between the two is possibly a common origin in the Christian communities of Asia Minor. E. Schüssler-Fiorenza defends the hypothesis that John and Revelation have some unique linguistic affinities which suggests that both might have emerged from a Christian "school" tradition in Asia Minor; see E. Schüssler-Fiorenza, *The Book of Revelation: Justice and Judgment* (Philadelphia: Fortress, 1985), 83–113. Both picture Christ as "lamb" and portray the reality of Christian worship as replacing the temple, for example. Schüssler-Fiorenza concludes that Revelation had access to primitive Johannine traditions, Pauline tradition and prophetic-apocalyptic material (p. 107).

5. The authors of *Mary in the New Testament* (pp. 235–36) conclude that it is not, since Revelation does not make such a secondary attribution here though it does do so elsewhere.

6. Identifying "Marys" present at the crucifixion by their sons was evidently an established part of the tradition (cf. Mk 15:40–41; Mt 27:56).

7. E.g. the beloved disciple's insight at the empty tomb (Jn 20:8) has no impact on the surrounding story, which develops along lines similar to its other versions (e.g. Lk 24:12, 22–24).

8. See G. Theissen, *The Miracle Stories of the Early Christian Tradition* (Philadelphia: Fortress, 1983), 103–06. Theissen notes that this class of miracle reflects a surprising, spontaneous abundance of material goods, rather than rescue from a threatening situation. The miracle may even be initiated by Jesus without intervention of others (e.g. Mk 6:35ff; 8:3), no miraculous technique is employed, and persons did not claim to perform such miracles as an index of special status.

9. Hence her absence until the crucifixion should not be overinterpreted (as in C.K. Barrett, *The Gospel According to St. John* [second ed.; Philadelphia: Westminster, 1978],

194, who presumes a period of private retirement prior to the real opening of Jesus' public ministry at Passover). John only mentions the disciples of Jesus during the public ministry when they are part of the underlying traditional material. John apparently wishes to dissociate Mary from the unbelieving "brothers" of Jesus (Jn 7:1–10), who do not recognize either Jesus' destined time (Greek *kairos*) or the testimony which he gives against the evil world. Sinaiticus omits "his disciples" from v. 12, perhaps under the influence of the synoptic tradition which makes both Mary and the brothers of Jesus outsiders to the circle of disciples.

10. R. Brown et al. (*Mary,* 187) point to this episode as a symbolic "follow-up" to the confessions of Jesus as messiah, since the promise of a messianic banquet is realized in the abundant gift of wine. This conclusion depends upon assuming that the gift of wine in itself would lead the readers of the gospel to think of wine as symbol of the messianic end-time (Hos 2:24; Jl 4:18; Is 29:17; Jer 31:5; *1 Enoch* 10:19; *2 Bar.* 29:5; see Schnackenburg, *John I,* 338.

11. See R. Bultmann, *The Gospel of John* (Philadelphia: Westminster, 1971 [Ger. 1964]), 113–14. For the view that the evangelist is responsible for the concluding half of the verse, see R. Schnackenburg (*The Gospel According to St. John,* Vol. 1 [New York: Herder & Herder, 1968]), 334.

12. See R. Brown, *The Gospel According to John I–XII* (Garden City: Doubleday, 1966), 100.

13. M.-E. Boismard, "Rapports entre foi et miracles entre l'Evangile de Jean," *EphTheoLouv* (1982), 357–64.

14. Boismard, "Foi et miracles," 362.

15. Schnackenburg, *John I,* 337.

16. R. Brown et al., *Mary,* 193–94.

17. See R. Brown, *The Gospel According to John XIII–XXI* (Garden City: Doubleday, 1971), 911–15.

18. Cf. R. Schnackenburg, *The Gospel According to John,* vol. 3 (New York: Crossroad, 1979), 323–27.

19. See Schnackenburg, *Gospel III,* 327.

20. See Schnackenburg, *John III*, 326.
21. See A. Collins, *The Combat Myth in the Book of Revelation* (HDR 9; Missoula: Scholars, 1976).
22. Ibid. 102–35.
23. Ibid. 136–38. The format divisions of the song involve: (a) proclaiming divine kingship (v. 10); (b) announcement of victory (v. 10); (c) description of victory (vv. 10–11); (d) summons to rejoice.
24. Ibid. 138–44.
25. R. Brown et al. (*Mary*, 237–39) finally reach the conclusion that any direct reference to Mary is excluded. Our earliest known mariological interpretations of the scene come from the fourth century.
26. On the problematic character of Revelation's ideal of a masculine ascetic/martyr untainted by contact with women (perceived as the cause of the fallen angels' lust) see A. Collins, "Women's History and Revelation," *Society of Biblical Literature 1987 Seminar Papers* (ed. K. Richards; Atlanta: Scholars, 1987), 84–90.
27. See apocryphal material such as *Gos. Hebr.* 1; *Acts of Paul* HSNTA 2:374–76; *Acts of Peter* HSNTA 2:306–307; *Sib. Or.* 8; HSNTA 2:740 (in R. Brown et al., *Mary*, 244–51).
28. *Gos. Heb.* 3; HSNTA 1:164; repeated in gnostic circles (e.g. *Gos. Phil.* 55:23; 59:6; 71:3; 73:8).
29. See J. Daniélou, *Gospel Message and Hellenistic Culture* (Philadelphia: Westminster, 1973), 158–59, 180–83.
30. Brown et al., *Mary*, 256.
31. E.g. the hymnic descent of divine Pronoia in *Apocry. Jn* CG II 30, 11–31, 25 or the shaking of the paths of the stars in *trim. Prot.* CG XIII 43, 4–30.
32. See W. Schoedel, *Ignatius of Antioch* (Philadelphia: Fortress, 1985), 90–92.
33. Cf. Tertullian, *Carn. Christ.* 23, 2–3; Schoedel, *Ignatius*, 90.
34. Schoedel, *Ignatius*, 62.
35. Ibid. 84–85.

Mary and the 'Anawim

Richard J. Sklba

Luke begins his gospel with a description of a mature encounter between Mary of Nazareth and the sovereign will of
God. The scene is usually entitled the annunciation, but the
narrative also possesses some elements of a prophetic call. At
the end of the dialogue with Gabriel, Mary states, "Behold the
servant/handmaid (*doule*) of the Lord" (Lk 1:38). The reference to the event as done "according to your word" contains a
subtle echo and reference to the great prophets of Israel whose
mission was to proclaim the word of Yahweh and to influence
by that very fact the unfolding of his dialogue with the poor.

PROPHETIC CALLINGS

Although the response of Mary may sound like the denoue-
ment of the story, or like the graceful relaxation of dramatic
tension after the highpoint of the angelic message, it is in fact
the literary climax of the dialogue. These words of Mary place
the story of the annunciation in continuity with another major
prophetic theme in Israel. We may recall the initial words of the
first of the servant songs woven into the text of Deutero-Isaiah.
An unknown prophetic leader in the exilic community is introduced and commissioned with the text which has become very
familiar to Christians, namely, "Here is my servant whom I
uphold, my chosen one with whom I am pleased" (Is 42:1).
Elsewhere the same mysterious exilic figure recalled that earlier

123

presentation in the midst of hidden preparation, " 'You are my servant,' he said to me" (Is 49:3). After suffering and triumph Yahweh is finally quoted as announcing, "Behold, my servant shall prosper; he shall be raised up and greatly exalted" (Is 52:13).

Confronted by an invitation which made no sense at all, perceiving the presence of Yahweh's power through the angelic message in an unexpected and unprecedented fashion, Mary of Nazareth took her place among Yahweh's servants, perhaps even among those prophets called to give word and witness to the hidden plan of God's salvific activity not yet seen by other members of the community of faith. She took her place among the poor who had no recourse except to respond, "Be it done to me according to your word" (Lk 1:38). Mary is presented as one who knows who she is with inner confidence and clarity. "Poor Mary," we say, never realizing how profound our comment really is!

In the Magnificat, when the same gospel places a song of praise on Mary's lips as she enters the home of Elizabeth, she acknowledges that God has "looked upon my lowliness (*tapeinosis*)" (Lk 1:48). The words of the canticle seem to celebrate her humble status and subordinate position in life by way of contrast to the exalted majesty of God. In so doing, the song of Mary echoes the life of Hagar who was once assured by an angelic messenger that "the Lord has heard of your lowliness" (Gen 16:11 where the Greek Septuagint strikingly used the word *tapeinosis* to translate the original Hebrew *'oni*). The words of Mary also echo the grateful acknowledgement of Leah, wife of Jacob, when, after the birth of Reuben, she announced, "The Lord has seen my lowliness" (Gen 29:32 where the very same combination of *tapeinosis* and *'oni* are found in their respective texts). Thus, by Mary's joyful gratitude toward God who "looked upon his handmaid's lowliness" (Lk 1:48), Luke seems deliberately to place Mary, not only among prophets, but also among women looked down upon by their peers and neighbors, among persons considered less significant, less socially respectable, less worthy of honor. The immediate context in each case was childbearing, but the end result was social contempt. Mary is depicted as entering the home of Elizabeth, as a servant of God who trusted the divine word and awaited God's salvific intervention which alone gave her dignity. Pausing there for a moment at the doorway of "Betty's house," she stood in solidarity with the prophets and the poor. She waited and she served.

The accounts of the annunciation and visitation present Mary with some traces of the prophetic tradition and we might wonder if the visitation itself is not a type of "prophetic action." Prophets often illustrated their messages and initiated divine action by their human deeds. The visitation thus becomes the first concrete illustration of the way God intends to deal with the world in a messianic age.

I may possess an overly creative imagination, but as I prepared for this symposium I suddenly realized that Père Gelin's book entitled *The Poor of Yahweh* (Liturgical Press: Collegeville, 1964) was translated from its third French edition into English just as the Second Vatican Council was exploring the mission of the church in the modern world (*Gaudium et Spes*), and just as Roman Catholics were seeking a more biblical understanding of Mary as a model for that church (*Lumen Gentium*, chapter 8). A servant church, open to the word of God and the needs of neighbor! What better mirror than Mary among God's poor?

THE PHILOLOGICAL ROOT AND MEANING OF 'ANAWIM

The root meaning of words can be fascinating. For example, what inner meaning gives us the right to call a factory a "plant"? I don't know. In another arena of life, I can explore the philological meaning of "obedience" as coming from the Latin *ob-audire*, to press one's ear against the wall, straining and eager for the slightest sound, ready to act on the first hint of conversation overheard. That type of investigation can provide profound illumination for the inner connection between hearing and obeying, and thus for the deeper significance of the latter. In particular, the study of Hebrew words can be positively intriguing. In that language all words sharing the same three central root letters are somehow interrelated in meaning.

It can become a challenge to detective work; it can also open up vast horizons of insight and understanding.

The Hebrew word *'anah* includes such root meanings as answer, being disposed to respond readily, as well as being somehow submissive to those who may demand an answer. One can easily understand how the same root word could mean inferior, lowly, humbled, even afflicted. The basic concept in this case seems to signify social relationship rather than distress or physical poverty. The adjective *'ani* refers to one who is subservient, listening, meek, lowly, not poor or destitute (as evidenced by the fact that the antonym in Hebrew for *'ani* would not be rich, but rather the range of words which signify dominant, powerful, violent, oppressive or abusive).

If Mary, by Luke's description, stands among the *'anawim,* she might have some money in the bank, but she has no political weight to throw around! She does the bidding of others. She awaits the command of another. The last word on the subject is not really her own. Thus we discover the deepest core of the conceptual link between prophets and the *'anawim:* they both listen carefully, by definition, seeking the divine will and God's plan from its first stirrings in the world around them.

If by extension the entire church stands among the *'anawim,* we don't pretend to possess political clout. We end up taking things on the chin more often than not; at least so it would seem in this day and age.

EXODUS AS A PARADIGM

In Egypt the Hebrews were on the bottom of any social heap one could imagine. They took orders from the pharaoh and all his appointees. They were clearly related as inferior to superior. They were dependent upon the word of those in control. They were *'anawim.*

Whatever happened at the exodus pried the Hebrews from their posture of subordination to the pharaoh, and gave them a new and freeing relationship—this time to Yahweh. Perhaps the Hebrews simply got sick and tired of the way things were. Perhaps they rose up in an early expression of solidarity like the shipyard workers of Gdansk. Perhaps groups of runaway slaves from Egypt banded together with pockets of revolting slaves in Canaan. Perhaps revolution was more the norm than military conquest. Whatever happened and however it occurred, the Hebrews gradually came to the understanding that it was Yahweh who had championed their cause and set them free. So they adopted a subordinate stance before their God and listened with new reverence to Yahweh. They became members of God's family, with all the dignity that relationship entailed, but they were always relatives who were somehow subordinate to their divine liberator. As such they were strictly commanded never to be abusive to one another. In particular, they were sternly warned not to mistreat those who were dependent in their midst, especially widows and orphans.

Laws were formulated to uphold and enforce mutual care and to avoid any traces of exploitation. "You shall not act violently against a stranger/resident refugee, nor oppress such a person, for you were strangers in Egypt yourselves. A widow or orphan you shall not reduce to subservience (*'anah*). If you push them down (*'anah*) so that they cry out to me, I will surely hear their cry of legal suit. My nostrils will flare with anger and I will kill you with the sword; your wives will be widows and your children orphans" (Ex 22:20–23; the translation is my own). In that social and political context widows and orphans were dependent on others for food and all basic human necessities, but Yahweh's people were forbidden to deal with them high-handedly. Yahweh was always on the side of those who were the underdogs. If they were in any way mistreated, Yahweh noted their lowliness, and promised to turn things around, sustaining and supporting their true dignity.

The exodus was a paradigm for everything. How did the Hebrews come to own the land of Canaan? Yahweh gave it to them as an inheritance because no one else would! Why were they freed from repeated oppression (*'anah*) in the accounts of the judges (Jgs 2:18)? Because Yahweh always frees, exalts and lifts up the afflicted and downcast! To obtain their rights, all the Hebrews need to do is once again assume the posture of respectful listeners (see Jer 7:21f). Moreover, in the theological

tradition familiarly named the Yahwist, Moses himself was chosen as leader; in relationship to Yahweh, he was truly "hum-
ble/respectful (*'ani*)," namely the most attentive, the most
responsive person among all the earthlings of creation (Num
11:3). Those who listen carefully are exalted and lifted up by
God. Moses stood among the *'anawim*. So did Mary.

USE IN CULT AND COURT

As Americans we take great pride in our independence and
value personal initiative highly. In the eighteenth century our
ancestors refused to be servants to England, and our nation has
welcomed millions of immigrants who shared the same senti-
ments. Admittedly, we were not very willing—shamefully resis-
tant in fact—to share the independence with our black sisters
and brothers but we surely relished our own freedom.

As a new cultural wave enters our society this decade, we
may hear an Hispanic refer to herself as "su servidora," and we
are tempted by our cultural bias to presume that the phrase is
mere courtesy. Turning to another part of the globe, we do not
really comprehend the fact that a devout Muslim could take
pride in the name Abdul, literally "servant of God." In our ears
it sounds too demeaning. However, in that regard we may be
the ones who are socially impoverished if our instinct for independence becomes translated into any subtle refusal to serve
others. The authors of the recent classic study of American
mores, *Habits of the Heart,* have documented this cultural flaw
and its inherent dangers. Unfortunately, if Mary of Nazareth
stands among the *'anawim*, she might not be among us today,
but rather only among those we look down upon.

By contrast, the faithful of Israel were truly proud to be
called servants of God. The psalms as music for worship referred to all participants as "servants (*'abadim*)." This was particularly true of the laments used to beg help for the poor,
needy and afflicted. A frequently recurring phrase includes the
self-description, "I am poor (*'ani*) and needy" (Pss 40:18, 86:1,
109:22). The theme of service is also found in the glorious
songs of praise (Pss 134:1, 135:1). Everyone praised the gran-

deur of God and felt privileged to be among Yahweh's servants who stood in respectful dependence upon their God, listening carefully to God's word.

Mary's self-identification as "servant/handmaid" (Lk 1:38) placed her in continuity, not only with the prophetic tradition, but also with that long line of temple worshipers who were proud to claim their dependence upon God.

PROPHETIC DEVELOPMENTS

In early Israel, at least judging from the similarity of homes uncovered from oldest levels of iron age cities in Palestine, there seems to have been a basic economic equality. Homes were alike, and little variation has been noted from one quarter of town to another. The new prosperity of both the northern kingdom of Israel as well as its southern counterpart of Judah during the eighth century B.C., however, seems to have changed everything. The famous ivories of Megiddo, publicly displayed at the Oriental Institute in Chicago, give clear testimony to the fact that some families began to possess an abundance of niceties. Some homes became very lovely indeed. In fact, a very elementary, but surprisingly effective method for selecting a promising site for archaeological excavation remains the "fresh air test." The most pleasant location for enjoying the prevailing breezes from the sea to the west will probably mark the spot on the Tell where ruins from the best homes will be found!

Beginning with Amos the prophets of Israel heard the voices of the poor in a new way, and raised their own voices in solidarity with them. Prophetic protest resulted from the increasingly clear perception that the prosperity of the nation was in fact built upon exploitation. Amos condemned the prosperous worshipers at Bethel for "panting after (literally, licking) the very dust on the heads of the poor and twisting the path of the *'anawim''* (Am 2:7), or for "gulping down the poor and bringing to a halt the 'anawim of the earth" (8:4). It still remains, after all these centuries, a very graphic manner of describing the greed and avarice of his day. Isaiah excoriated those who "grind the faces of the poor" (Is 3:15), and Micah became positively ghoulish in describing those who "pluck off the skin of the people, strip the bones of meat, take the bones and make stew of the people" (Mic 3:2–3).

These same prophets spoke in scathing terms of the worship in the temple, because although it was intended to symbolize a people united in dependence on Yahweh, it became all too often in fact the occasion for self-exaltation and boasting. Human accomplishments, rather than the great deeds of Yahweh's redemptive action, were celebrated. Though all were supposed to be lowly and humble before God, some were a great deal lower than others, and in the judgment of the great prophets were kept in that situation by injustice and violence.

Did the prophets of the eighth century B.C. influence the final formulation of Deuteronomy's legislation, or did the laws provide an impetus for these prophets, or were the consciences of several groups raised at the same time in history? We are not able to make certain judgments in the area of historical development. We do not know. I suspect that, as in most historical movements, the groups were in fact influenced by each other. We do know that the new laws surfaced, such as that of forbidding the overnight retention of a coat taken in pledge (Dt 24:12) or the abuse of a hired servant (24:14) or the withholding of payment from one day to the next (24:15). All the laws underscored the common conviction that people ought not be demeaned in these newly improvised ways, nor kept in abject dependence. Perhaps some folks were low, but they should not be kept that way.

Perhaps it was Zephaniah in the seventh century B.C. who most clearly described the lowly as a metaphor for authentic spiritual health. His intention was not that people should be physically poor, but rather that they (and all the people of Judah) should view everything as a gift. In the eyes of Zephaniah, possessions were not really earned nor merited, but simply received. "Seek the Lord, all you lowly (*'anawim*) of the earth; seek lowliness (*'anawah*)" (Zeph 2:3). "I will leave in your midst a people lowly (*'ani*) and poor; they will trust in the name of the Lord" (3:12).

In the midst of such a people stood Mary of Nazareth, without pretense or claim to personal achievement, able to be used by God for purposes beyond her wildest dreams, not exploiting others, but rather listening to her God as attentively as possible.

INTERTESTAMENTAL DEVELOPMENTS

Judah experienced one wave of foreign domination after another, first Babylonian, then Persian, then Greek and finally Roman. It was almost inevitable that a figure like Judah Maccabee would eventually arrive on the scene to stir up military resistance. It was inevitable, yet ever under the guidance of God's Spirit, that those who spun tales after supper would reach back into the glorious past to find elements for tales of yet another king who would come with soldiers beyond count and weapons beyond defeat. Another David, yes, that's it, another David! But not everyone spoke of armies more powerful than those of the fabled ancient Egyptians or Assyrians. Some remembered the lowliness and meekness of Moses. Some remembered David before he became so high-minded, when he rode on a white mule to be anointed and crowned. Zechariah was such a one, calling out, "Rejoice, daughter of Zion, for your king comes, lowly (*'ani*) and seated on a donkey" (Zech 9:9).

Still later those at Qumran would speak of the community of the poor; in fact it seems to have been their favorite title. The phrase asserted that God would do the work and supply the power; all they had to do was keep mind and heart open and ready.

Was there a distinctive movement at that time, similar to that of our current contemporaries who join Pax Christi to testify to the importance of peace and non-violence today? I don't know. Père Gelin seems to think so. He and many others would claim that members of such a movement would sing Psalms 9 and 10 whenever they gathered (almost like a regular third order meeting). Scholars wonder if the Magnificat itself might not have been one of the popular spirituals of that day, almost equivalent to the popularity of the Saint Louis Jesuits of our age. Whatever the merits of such a theory, there were undoubtedly many who expected the final redemption of Israel, some like the Zealots with revolutionary daggers to assist the cause, others like the Essenes out in the desert armed only with ritual purity. Still others, like Simeon and Anna (Lk 2:25–38), suspected that God would surprise them all; so they joined the *'anawim* and stood and waited.

Understanding Mary of Nazareth in This Light

Mary was truly among the *'anawim,* and addressed as such by the angel who came, not to her alone, but "to a town of Galilee called Nazareth" (Lk 1:26). In the midst of her people, she was acknowledged as radically dependent upon the sovereign will of God. She was open to new beginnings, living with the unexpected, enthralled by the presence of God, reaching out in service to those around, to the human needs of ordinary folks because they were all bound together by the grace of God in history. Mary of Nazareth is a model for the church. Luke made her a paradigm for the way God's salvation works.

Mary is among the *'anawim,* and God does great things for her and for them every time!

The Justice Dimension: Mary as Advocate of Peace

Carol Frances Jegen

If Mary of Nazareth were presented with a title which included both the dimension of justice and advocacy for peace, perhaps her mind and heart would immediately respond with the promising words of Psalm 85, "Justice and peace shall kiss." Attuned as she must have been to the beautiful psalmody of her Jewish heritage, Mary would have recalled other verses of that covenantal psalm:

> I will hear what God proclaims;
>   the Lord—for he proclaims peace
> To his people, and to his faithful ones
>   and to those who put in him their hope.
> Near indeed is his salvation to those who fear him,
>   glory dwelling in our land.
> Kindness and truth shall meet;
>   justice and peace shall kiss.
> Truth shall spring out of the earth,
>   and justice shall look down from heaven.

Today's scripture scholars vary in their interpretation of this psalm as far as its timing and setting are concerned, but they do agree on the major thrust of this prayer. Psalm 85 praises God's past fidelity and consequently awakens hope with respect to the future. The prominent biblical scholar Artur Weiser commented on Psalm 85's powerful spiritual message in the following words: ". . . this is the faith that has prevented the religious values of the (Hebrew scriptures) from being utterly defeated by the manifold obstacles raised in the course of history by the actual state of affairs on earth."[1]

Mary, identified in the Lucan annunciation scene as the "servant of the Lord" (Lk 1:38), must have been familiar also with the strong justice themes in the Isaian servant theology. Yahweh's own spirit had been given to the servant so that justice would be brought to the nations (Is 42:1). The servant was called to establish justice on the earth. Even the far-away coastlands would wait for the servant's teaching (Is 42:4). Yahweh called and formed the servant for the victory of justice (Is 42:6). Mary knew the whole story of the Isaian servant, culminating in a love unto suffering and death. Mary also must have known how the early church began to understand Jesus as Yahweh's holy servant (Acts 3:13, 26; 4:30), the one bringing true justice and genuine peace.[2]

As the liturgical prayer of the early Jewish-Christian community developed, Mary quite likely was familiar with the song of Zachariah, eventually inserted into the Lucan gospel and commonly referred to in later years as the Benedictus. There, too, Mary would have been mindful of the ways in which justice and peace themes were related, this time in the image of the rising sun. When the dawn from on high was applied to her own son, Jesus, who would guide his disciples' feet into the ways of peace (Lk 1:79), Mary, along with other Jewish-Christian worshipers, could have recalled readily the rising sun imagery of the prophet Malachi. This prophet promised a sun with healing rays of justice. In beautiful ways of prayer familiar to Mary, once again justice and peace kissed, this time in the image of the rising sun, the dayspring from on high.[3]

To us, who probably are not quite so attuned to the justice/peace imagery of a Hebraic thought world, a contemporary statement relating peace with justice might more readily come to mind. How often we use the statement of Paul VI, "If you want peace, work for justice." And the more we have become active in any one of the myriad struggles for justice and the almost overwhelming efforts for peace, you and I know from experience that justice and peace are integrally related. Either we find ways for justice and peace to kiss, or we will experience neither.

As we approach the final decade of this twentieth century, the intrinsic relation between justice and peace is apparent in the global struggles in which the entire human community is involved. Significantly these life/death conflicts are referred to in global terms of east/west and north/south tensions. Those of the east and west, focused primarily on the rivalries between the two superpowers, the Soviet Union and the United States, are tensions of war and peace. These nations are superpowers primarily because they have nuclear weapons capable of unimaginable destruction and death.

North/south tensions refer to the tragic relations between the rich nations of the north and the poor nations of the south. Consequently, the north/south conflict is seen to be primarily one of justice. However, the more one penetrates into the causes of injustice and the lack of peace in the third world, the more one sees in our own times how justice and peace cannot be separated. Who could even begin to calculate the escalation of war in some of the poorest countries of the world, including those of Central America, because conflicting ideologies of east and west have been insidiously and falsely inserted into the north/south struggles for justice and for basic human rights?

At the second international, ecumenical conference, "Toward a Theology of Peace," held in Budapest in December 1987, the Jesuit Luis Aguirre from Uruguay spoke of east/west, north/south tensions in words I could never forget. Addressing the entire assembly, Father Aguirre stated:

> Our major objective, yours and mine, is the stopping of the escalation of nuclear weapons and the feeding of the world's hungry who starve because vital resources are diverted to militarism and to the arms race.
>
> But we may discover a significant difference.

Your urgent task is to prevent a *possible genocide* in the first world. My urgent task is to halt the *actual genocide* in the third world.

Today, by midnight, as each day, in the sight of our frightened eyes, more than 45,000 of our children will be dead, because of malnutrition and starvation. And for each child dead, more than 245,000 will continue to live in precarious conditions for the rest of their lives, marked in their minds and bodies by illness. Our poor countries are victims of the violence of the debt crisis. $2 million per minute is paid out in interest on a total world debt of $20 trillion, even more than the $1.5 million per minute spent on militarism. And at the same time almost each second a child is dying of hunger.[4]

One day during that conference, Father Aguirre and I discussed some of the issues he raised in his paper. He described some of his work with abandoned children and claimed that the situation of children in Latin America is almost impossible for the human imagination to grasp. He said the Brazilian government admits that 34 million children roam the streets of that country alone. The real number of abandoned children there is even greater. And we of the north, in the name of promoting democracy, continue to send to the south more and more ammunitions and less and less human aid.

The Budapest Peace Theology Conference took place during Advent. People were there from all over the world—South Africa, Uganda, the Philippines, Indonesia, New Zealand, India, Uruguay, Nicaragua, Mexico, western and eastern Europe, including the Soviet Union, Canada and the United States. Each midday the entire group, Anglicans, Protestants, Orthodox, and Roman Catholics, gathered around an Advent shrine of Mary and prayed for the peace of the world. In front of Mary's shrine, the women from Great Britain had placed a piece of wire from Greenham Common. Our prayer together was a continual reminder that justice and peace must kiss in our world. Together we knew that somehow Mary would help us find ways to justice and walk the ways of peace.

In our own United States, the struggle for justice is becoming more and more related to non-violent, peacemaking approaches. One of the most significant and most persistent of these efforts is that of the United Farm Workers under the faith-filled leadership of Cesar Chavez. For more than two decades Cesar Chavez, following in the footsteps of Mohandas Gandhi and Martin Luther King, Jr., has led the farmworkers' struggle for justice against almost unbelievable odds. Today that struggle continues in a non-violent way.

Anyone familiar with the non-violent efforts of the United Farm Workers knows that Mary plays a most prominent role. The banner of Our Lady of Guadalupe is displayed proudly and confidently at all major United Farm Worker events. The headquarters of the union, a converted tuberculosis sanitarium in southern California, is usually referred to as La Paz. However, its proper identification is Nuestra Señora de la Paz, Our Lady of Peace.

This past spring Cesar Chavez addressed a group of students and other farmworker supporters at Loyola University in Chicago. In reply to a question from the audience regarding a recent lawsuit of several million dollars levied against the farmworkers, Cesar uttered a profound statement of faith. He declared unhesitatingly that God would see them through. "After all," he remarked, "it's a miracle that we even exist." In the coming National Assembly of Pax Christi USA, Cesar Chavez will be one of the major speakers. The significant testimony of the United Farm Workers to the kiss of justice and peace in our land is an unexplainable phenomenon without their sincere, constant devotion to Mary.

More than once I have suggested that long-standing devotion to Mary among various ethnic groups in our country can be a key factor in undoing some of the tensions and rivalries which undermine justice and make peace impossible in so many of our local communities and even in some of our parishes. For example, our Mexican people with their beautiful devotion to

Our Lady of Guadalupe can relate almost instinctively to our Polish Catholics' profound devotion to Our Lady of Czesto-chowa. And recently, in an article entitled "Mary, Woman for Our World" (*Chicago Studies,* April 1988), I highlighted the significance of the renowned Russian icon, Our Lady of Vladi-mir, along with the Mexican portrayal of Our Lady of Guada-lupe, in the context of resolving east/west, north/south tensions through genuine devotion to Mary.

Such an approach to Mary's role in today's global struggles for justice and peace resonates well with the thrust of *Redemp-toris Mater,* the encyclical of John Paul II calling us to this Marian Year in preparation for the year 2000. As mother of the Americas, Our Lady of Guadalupe reminds us also of 1992, the five hundredth anniversary of the discovery of America. Such a reminder is not without its heartache if we face honestly the brutal exploitation of the native peoples of the Americas, an exploitation which continues to this very day.

To be serious about justice and peace with Mary means to be plunged into the mystery of suffering. In our own bishops' pastoral letter, *The Challenge of Peace,* Mary is mentioned explic-itly in the final, pastoral section of the document. In some ways the placement of the Marian references in this peace pastoral parallels the climactic position of the Marian teachings of Vati-can II as we find them in the final chapter of *Lumen Gentium.* There we can turn to Mary to see what it means to live *in* the mystery of Christ and the church. In the peace document's concluding section, we are urged to pray to Mary, queen and lady of peace, who is the first disciple of Jesus. But in the first section of this pastoral letter, we begin to see what it means to be a disciple of Jesus the peacemaker. There we are reminded that Jesus is our peace, as pertinent texts from the epistle to the Ephesians are quoted (CP 20). This epistle minces no words about the reconciling action of Jesus. He is our peace because he shed his blood on a cross (Eph 2:13f). As first disciple, Mary shared Jesus' peacemaking agony as no other person could.

Today's peacemaking challenge in a world writhing in the agonies of injustice calls us to the mystery of Calvary. In all honesty we must ask ourselves where we are standing on that hill of crucifixion. Are we with Mary entering into the agony of her son in ways of active, compassionate presence? Or could it be that we are part of the mob crucifying Jesus again?

Archbishop Raymond Hunthausen boldly has applied crucifixion imagery to the arms race. In unforgettable words he decried our nuclear madness when he cried out as prophet:

> Our nuclear war preparations are the global crucifixion of Jesus. What we do to the least of these, through our nuclear war planning, we do to Jesus. This is his teaching. We cannot avoid it and we should not try. Our nuclear weapons are the final crucifixion of Jesus, the extermination of the human family with whom he is one.[5]

The year 1987 recorded a new high in global military expenditures at $1.8 million a minute.[6] This new high is often justified through the doctrine of deterrence. In June 1988, Catholic bishops will meet to discuss their new statement on deterrence. Pax Christi USA has sent out a new call for fasting and prayer that the bishops will unhesitatingly condemn this doctrine which is responsible for untold suffering on the part of the poor of the world. Vatican II cautioned us in *Gaudium et Spes* that "the arms race is an utterly treacherous trap for humanity, and one which injures the poor to an intolerable degree. It is much to be feared that if this race persists, it will eventually spawn all the lethal ruin whose path it is now making ready" (GS 81). If such a statement could be made over twenty years ago, what must be said now when "the nuclear bomb inventories of the two superpowers, already sufficient to destroy all life on earth many times over, increased in 1987 at the rate of 16 per week."[7] "The megatonnage, or destructive force, in today's nuclear stockpile corresponds to at least one million Hiroshima-size bombs; is 2,667 times the deadly energy released in World War II; provides the equivalent of 3.2 tons of TNT for everyone on earth."[8] This is where deterrence has led us. How can these present conditions possibly be considered morally acceptable?

In 1987 Bishop Thomas Gumbleton, President of Pax Christi USA, delivered an address at Seton Hall University which was later reprinted in part in the June–July 1987 issue of *The Catholic Worker* under the title "The Sin of Deterrence." Bishop Gumbleton straightforwardly focused on the issue of the *intention to use* the weapons which are stockpiled in a balance of terror under the rubric of nuclear deterrence. Reporting on interviews with military personnel who are on alert at United States missile sites on land and on nuclear submarines, Bishop Gumbleton documented the official government policy of intent to use so-called "deterring" weapons. In the words of one retired officer quoted in the article, "If the responsibility fell to me, I fully intended to destroy the Soviet Union."[9] When one tries to consider the magnitude of evil in such a statement with respect to hundreds of millions of human lives, one is hard pressed to find words to describe such a sin. Yet this intent to kill is the present policy of a nation whose patroness is Mary Immaculate.

On December 8, 1987, the feast of the Immaculate Conception, a most extraordinary event took place in the signing of the INF treaty. Perhaps no one caught the significance of this event for the history of the human family better than Mikhail Gorbachev, who stated:

> May December 8, 1987, become a date that will be inscribed in the history books—a date that will mark the watershed separating the era of a mounting risk of nuclear war from the era of a demilitarization of human life.

The INF treaty is the first small step in the undoing of deterrence. Was it mere coincidence that this treaty was signed in the United States on our patronal feast day, the feast of the Immaculate Conception? The symbolism so often used for the immaculate conception is that of a woman triumphing over the evil encircling the world. May this symbolism take on new meaning for us as we ponder the significance of the date on which the INF treaty was signed.[10]

Not only in 1987, but in other recent years as well, the feast of the Immaculate Conception has acquired new significance for the peacemaking efforts of the church. Paul VI chose this feast in 1967 to announce the inauguration of the first worldwide Day of Peace to be celebrated annually on January 1, the feast of Mary's Motherhood and the beginning of a new year. The Day of Peace is designated as a day of universal prayer for peace.

On December 8, 1971, following the synod which gave us the renowned document *Justice in the World,* Paul VI issued his invitation to celebrate the 1972 Day of Peace on which the inseparable relation between justice and peace was to be highlighted. Characterizing the contemporary understanding of justice as a "dynamic justice," he presented his "incisive and dynamic formula: 'If you want peace, work for justice.' " This was the message promulgated on the feast of Mary's Immaculate Conception.

MARY IMMACULATE, THE KISS OF JUSTICE AND PEACE

Thus far we have addressed Mary's likely familiarity with some of the ways her own Hebrew scriptures spoke of the integral relation between justice and peace. We have also considered some of the ways the mutual interaction of justice and peace is emphasized today in the global tensions of east and west, north and south. We have referred to some Marian devotions which speak directly to these global issues. It is appropriate now to turn directly to Mary herself and suggest that Mary *is* the kiss of justice and peace in the mystery of her immaculate conception.

Both justice and peace can be described and defined in various ways. When we begin to consider the meaning of Mary's immaculate conception, perhaps the word justification comes to mind more readily than the word justice. In our theological heritage, the many volumes written on justification could lead one to wonder if justification has much, if anything, to do with justice in the social order. Any consideration of Mary's immaculate conception in relation to justice and peace might seem, at

first sight, to move the discussion into the area of justification and away from the contemporary emphasis on justice
and peace.

In that wonderful volume *The Faith That Does Justice* edited
by John Haughey a decade ago, two essays are particularly
helpful in our reflections on Mary: "Biblical Perspectives on
Justice" by John R. Donahue and "Tridentine Justification and
Justice" by Richard R. Roach. In those essays we learn that "the
biblical idea of justice can be described as *fidelity to the demands
of a relationship.*"[11] Justification is explained as "participation in
the justice of God for his creation."[12] Both essays emphasize
that biblical justice and theological justification speak to the
societal order as well as to the personal order of reality. But
what do these insights into justification and justice have to do
with Mary's immaculate conception? How do these contemporary considerations of justice and justification speak to the
question of peace?

The pastoral letter *The Challenge of Peace: God's Promise and
Our Response* indicates briefly the variety of ways in which peace
is understood. There peace is described in terms of personal
security, the cessation of armed hostility, a right relationship
with God, and eschatological peace.[13] For our present delibera-
tion it is significant that *peace* is presented in terms of a right
relationship with God. In recent theological writings such as
Donahue's essay, *justice* also is described in terms of relationship with an emphasis on fidelity. In the context of a relationship with God characterized by both justice and peace, a
relationship which truly witnesses to a mutual fidelity in love,
we can glimpse something of the wondrous beauty of Mary's
immaculate conception.

In whatever way we may choose to gain insight into the
mystery of Mary's immaculate conception, including the kiss of
justice and peace, we need to be reminded that the same mystery of God's love at work in Mary is also at work in us. Karl
Rahner places great emphasis on our oneness with Mary in the
mystery of her son's redeeming action. In the book *Mary According to Women,* a publication resulting from the 1983 Mary
Festival at Mundelein College in Chicago, my article follows

Rahner's lead in a consideration of Mary's immaculate conception as a mystery of freedom.[14] It would take another study to probe more thoroughly into the intrinsic relations present in the gifts of justice, peace, and freedom bestowed on Mary and on us continually by an infinitely faithful and loving God. But at this point, let it suffice to say that whatever else a kiss might mean, including the kiss of justice and peace, such a kiss must be an expression of freedom, because a kiss is an expression of love.

From the first moment of Mary's existence, she began a relationship with God which intensified in love throughout her life. Mary, the justified one, participated ever more completely in God's justice for all creation. Her relation to each person witnessed to God's own justice and reconciling peace. As we know from her Magnificat, Mary's justice was an active justice, aware of the need to undo the injustices suffered by the hungry and poor of the world.

The kiss of justice and peace in Mary was continually sealed by her prayerfulness, her great pondering of heart. There her oneness in God intensified. In prayer Mary was strengthened to guide both her young son Jesus and his young Pentecost community into the ways of peace.

Theological significance always depends on genuine human experience. Mary Immaculate can be called queen of peace, lady of peace, advocate for peace because she was and is the first disciple of Jesus. Mary's agony on Calvary, Mary's faith in Easter, and Mary's prayerful forgiveness at Pentecost make her the woman of peace for all times. In each mystery of her life, Mary was faithful to her loving relationship with God. In each mystery of Jesus' life, Mary was faithful to her loving relationship with her Son.

Mary shared the sufferings of Jesus, not only on Calvary, but all through his life. As her compassionate, immaculate heart was broken open by suffering, God's own love empowered Mary to move into the mystery of Pentecost, not just once, but in every Pentecost in the church's history.

This Marian Year comes in our time of a new pentecost. But our time is also a time of demonic power for death. As advocate for peace, Mary calls us to share the suffering of her children all over the world. Mary calls us to be prayerful people of genuine compassion, fired by the Spirit of her son, that same Spirit who spoke through the prophets of Mary's people, that same Spirit who empowered the first Christians with martyr-dom love.

As advocate for peace, Mary calls each of us to be genuine disciples of Jesus, following her in his way of love even into suffering unto death. Mary calls us to live in such a way that God's own justice and peace shall kiss in our lives as well as in hers. Mary's prayer for us and Mary's challenge to us is that justice and peace shall kiss in our world.

Notes

1. Artur Weiser, *The Psalms* (Philadelphia: Westminster, 1976), 571.
2. For a consideration of the Isaian servant theology in rela-tion to the peacemaking ways of Jesus, see Carol Frances Jegen, BVM, *Jesus the Peacemaker* (Kansas City: Sheed & Ward, 1986), Ch. 3, "Prayer of Peacemakers."
3. Ibid. Ch. 4, "Preludes to Peacemaking." Here is given a more extensive development of the justice and peace themes in the Lucan canticles.
4. Luis Perez Aguirre, "Towards a Theology of Peace through the Power of the Poor," in *Preparatory Papers: Towards a Theology of Peace* (Budapest: Raday College, 1987), 57.
5. As quoted in *Jesus the Peacemaker*, 51.
6. Ruth Leger Sivard, *World Military and Social Expenditures 1987–88* (Washington, DC: World Priorities, 1987), 5.
7. Ibid.
8. Ibid. 16.
9. Thomas J. Gumbleton, "The Sin of Deterrence," *The Catholic Worker* LIV, 4, June–July 1987, 4.
10. As quoted in Carol Frances Jegen, BVM, "Mary: Woman for Our World," *Chicago Studies* 27, 1, April 1988, 59.

11. John C. Haughey, ed., *The Faith That Does Justice* (New York: Paulist Press, 1977), 69.
12. Ibid. 185.
13. *The Challenge of Peace* (Washington, DC: National Conference of Catholic Bishops, 1983), #27.
14. Carol Frances Jegen, BVM, "Mary Immaculate: Woman of Freedom, Patroness of the United States," in Carol Frances Jegen, BVM, ed., *Mary According to Women* (Kansas City: Sheed & Ward, 1985), especially 149f.

Mary and Evangelization in the Americas

Virgil Elizondo

In the third millennium of Christianity Mary may be a great source of ecumenical unity, beyond our present wildest imaginations. Far from being an obstacle to unity, Mary may become the ultimate source of unity. Events occurring around the world give indications of this. One of the most fascinating topics growing out of those events is the role of Mary in the evangelization of the Americas. This paper will address that topic, specifically Mary as she appeared in Guadalupe and Tepeyac and started—and continues today—the evangelization of Mexico.

As a pastor, whether I believe it or not and whether I like it or not, I cannot deny the massive and growing devotion to Our Lady of Guadalupe, not only among Mexicans but among people throughout the Americas. This devotion started in 1531, but, rather than diminishing, it is continuing to grow. One of the largest celebrations of the shrine of the Immaculate Conception in Washington is the feast of Our Lady of Guadalupe. It far surpasses the feast of the Immaculate Conception itself. We see growing devotion not only among church people but among people who have no relation to the church. We see it among artists and among poets as we saw it in young men going to war in Vietnam. They were afraid that they might lose their medals, so they had the image of Our Lady tattooed over their heart so they would not lose her as they went to battle.

Whether I believe in this or not, it imposes itself upon me as a pastor. I cannot disregard the massive expression of faith of the people of God. I would be a fool to deny it and I would be pastorally irresponsible to deny it. On the other hand, I have no trouble believing it. I grew up in a tradition for whom devotion to Our Lady was second nature. And therefore it is part of my tradition—part of who I am—to be able to relate intimately with Mary as a compassionate mother. When no one else understands, she understands. When no one else is around to listen, she is around to listen. When no one will support and motivate, she will support and motivate. And so devotion to Mary is a very real part of who I am as a man, as a Christian, as a Catholic in the twentieth century.

The appearance of Mary at Tepeyac in 1531 was far more than just a Marian apparition. It was one of the most exciting interventions of God in the history of Christianity—a direct intervention of God at a moment of history that will never be repeated. We need to situate ourselves at that historical moment to appreciate the power of what happened and to see that what was started has yet to come to completion.

At the end of the 1400s, there was a mass movement of Europeans seeking to find new routes to the far east. In the process they stumbled upon a plot of land that they thought was India. They named the natives Indians without stopping to ask them who they were or listening to what they called themselves. That mistake is symbolic of the encounter between two worlds that had not suspected the existence of each other. It began the massive encounter of the western world with what today we call the Americas. The beginning is fascinating, but it is equally painful. The encounter is centered in Mexico, beginning symbolically on Good Friday of the year 1519. The city where Cortez landed is called De La Cruz because he landed on the day of the cross. That started the prolonged Good Friday that is still being lived today by much of Latin America and by the native Americans.

In the beginning there was a mutual fascination between the Spaniards and the natives. They could not understand each other and yet they were fascinated with the robes, the dress, the foods, the customs, and even the religion. But the fascination quickly turned into fear and fear quickly turned into a battle. The battle was, in effect, a first world war—the first war that happened between the world they would call the "New World" and the world they would call "Old Europe." It was a bitter war. There were massive casualties. The massacre of native Mexican men and the rape of Mexican women were wholesale. Their cities and their temples were destroyed; their whole society was crushed and came to an end. That is the beginning of Mexico. It is a painful beginning—a beginning of conquest, of bloodshed, of robbery, of rape, of violence, of the end.

It was into this situation that the missionaries came. They were great men of the gospel—great men of the pre-reformation renewal movements of Europe. They had been influenced by Erasmus of Rotterdam, who already was initiating a return to the sources of Christianity in the gospels. They were so evangelical that the Latin American bishops were prohibited from taking part in the Council of Trent because they were considered to be too much like Protestants.

Place yourself for a moment in the position of the conquered people. They had been devastated. Everything that was of value to them had been destroyed. And now the missionaries of the God of the conquistadors, missionaries who were very holy and saintly men, came in and began to proclaim a gospel of love, of compassion, and of forgiveness. The people could not understand them. They were the missionaries of the same group that just slaughtered the people and they practiced the same religion. When the priests spoke about love and compassion and understanding and generosity, the people could not comprehend. How could these men speak of a God so opposite from their experience?

At that moment in history the Mexican nation had a collective death wish. They no longer wanted to live. They wanted only to die. When you study the Indian poetry of the immediate post-conquest era, it sounds like the psalms of lamentation, the painful psalms of the exile—"My God, my God, why have you abandoned me?" The people would sing to the missionaries: You have slaughtered our men, you have raped our women, you have destroyed our temples and our cities, and now you tell us that our gods are not true. If what you say is true, then why live? Let us die.

That was the prayer of the people. Collectively they had no reason to live. Everything of value to them had been wiped out and now they were told that even their gods were false. The first missionaries had prepared themselves to present the gospel in the best possible way to the theologians of the Indian nations. These were the first ecumenical dialogues between the theologians of Europe and the theologians of the Indian nations. They are called "los coloquios de las doce" because there were twelve. This was a new apostolic college coming to start a new church in a new millennium. They had given up on the European church. They thought it was so corrupt that there was no chance for renewal. The new church would now begin in the Americas. But communication was not easy. The Indian priests would say to them: "Look, you tell us all these things about our gods. But our gods have given us life. Our gods have given us sustenance. Our gods have led us to build our cities. Our gods have led us to build our value systems. And now you tell us that our gods are false. But our gods are not here to defend themselves. How can we betray them? We cannot believe you." At the rational level, the missionaries were not able to communicate. At a psychological level they were not able to pierce through the pain and the agony that the people had been experiencing. The missionaries included people like Bartolome de las Casas, the great Dominican who crossed the ocean thirteen times to speak in defense of the Indians. And Pedro de Gant dedicated his life to learning the language of the Indians and in the 1520s composed the first catechism totally in Indian hieroglyphics. The history of catechetics says that Martin Luther wrote the first popular catechism of the people. I believe the first popular catechism was written in the Americas by Pedro de Gant. It includes the creed, the commandments, and the virtues, all in one catechism written for the common people.

In some ways the missionaries were the agents of the ultimate violence because they were the agents of religious violence. There is nothing deeper for people than their religious roots—their god-imagery. When the chosen people were slaves in Egypt, the first thing they asked was to worship in their own way. Nothing is deeper for people than that.

Recently I was in Germany doing some workshops for the Spanish-speaking military, discussing Hispanic-United States relations within the military. We had a good discussion—all in English. Everyone spoke English perfectly. Toward the end of the meeting a woman raised her hand tentatively and I asked if she wanted to say something. She said, "Well, no, maybe not. Maybe not really." I said, "Go ahead, what did you want to say?" She said, "Well, I'm sort of embarrassed to say it but I really want to ask, since the time is almost over, would you lead us in saying a 'Hail Mary' in Spanish?" I said, "Certainly." So we all got up and said a "Dios te salve Maria" in Spanish. A number of people started to cry. Several came up afterward and said that it was the deepest religious experience they had ever had since being in the military.

Never underestimate the power of our core religious imagery, of our core religious symbolism. Theology is second level —at the head level. At the gut level, what imagery puts me in communion with my God? At this level the missionaries, without intending to be, were the agents of the ultimate violence, defending the people but doing violence among them by uprooting the images of their gods.

And so the conquest brought about a fourfold oppression of the people. One, it initiated a political and economic oppression that has continued until this day. It instituted political and economic structures that worked in favor of the conquistadors and against the conquered. And in spite of all the independence movements in Latin American nations, things have not changed. Whoever is at the top of the pyramid has the power, whether it is Europeans or the Latin American rich. The masses of Latin American poor have remained poor, whether they are a colonial state or a free state. Nothing has changed.

The same is true for many of the Mexican-American poor in the southwest United States. When slavery was eliminated after the Civil War, the Mexican-American poor became more desirable to the landowners than the slaves. It was more economical to rent people and discard them when you were finished with them than to own them. And so the Latin American poor in the southwest United States took the place of the slaves after the Civil War. Political and economic oppression continues to this day.

There was also sexual oppression from the beginning in the way the poor women were taken over and abused sociologically and sexually—the phenomenon of the absent father, the soldiers coming through and impregnating the women and going on, the beginning of what Octavio Paz, the great philosopher-poet of Mexico, has called "De La Chingala." The women were raped and then insulted and called whores. But equally evil and perhaps even more destructive has been the sexual oppression of the poor Latin American males. There is nothing more oppressive and destructive for the male than to see the female being abused and not be able to do anything about it. There is nothing more castrating and destructive to the male psyche than being forced to see that which he respects and admires the most being degraded and oppressed and abused and not be able to do anything about it. The classic movie "El Topo," a Spanish movie, shows precisely what happens when the poor women are abused and the men are physically forced to watch it but not allowed to do anything about it. Sexual oppression of both men and women began with the conquest and continues to our day.

Social and psychological oppression has resulted from the debates over whether the Indians were human or not. When all the great theologians and philosophers decided that the Indian was indeed human, the first provincial council of Mexico decided that they may be human but they were minors and therefore had not obtained the age of reason. One of the reasons we have a shortage of vocations in Latin American countries is because the church called them minors and did not allow them the sacrament of holy orders. And so consistently the wise men and women of that tradition were relegated to permanent positions of inferiority. In Latin America, if you want to insult someone you call him an "Indio." The social and psychological oppression continues. On Mexican soap operas you will see this same dynamic. Who is in power and who is below? Brown-skinned Indian mulattos are the maids, the sweepers, and the taxi-drivers. The blondes (whether it is false or true blonde) are the ones who have wealth and power. Religious communities also follow this color-coding in choosing superiors. They have been told that if they have Indians as superiors they will not get vocations. The church has not been immune to the social and psychological oppression which exists in the culture.

Finally, there has been religious oppression because the missionaries came to convert by total opposition: my religious expression against yours. Anything they could not understand was labeled as diabolical and had to be wiped out. The natives and the mestizos had to practice the religion of the oppressor in the way the oppressor determined. And so religion—official, institutional religion—was part of the ongoing oppression of the masses of poor in Latin America.

Into that setting comes an incredible eruption of God's goodness. It always happens that way. The God of the Bible, as Raymond Brown has said so beautifully, is always the God of unexpected surprises—the God that comes through in a way that we could only begin to suspect or imagine. It was an incredible surprise that the Son of God would become flesh as a Galilean. Everyone knew that nothing good could come out of Galilee. The God of the Bible is always the God that acts in ways that you and I can only begin to imagine or suspect. And once again, in the midst of this incredible hell of suffering created through our own efforts to conquer and become great at the cost of others, the God of goodness, the God of the Bible, the God who hears the cries of the poor, the God of the exodus, the God who sees the suffering of the afflicted, and the God who says, "I am going to save my people"—that God made an eruption.

The worst battle of the conquest took place in 1521. During the following years the people wanted only to die. Now in 1531, only ten years later, in the context of a massive death wish, this incredible eruption of God takes place in such a simple way that it is reminiscent of the birth narratives of the gospels of Jesus.

A simple Indian—not just an Indian but the lowest class Indian—was walking to church where he was a catechumen, and he heard beautiful music. He heard such beautiful singing that he thought he had died and was awakening in paradise. In the Indian world, life is a dream and death is the awakening. So he thought that he had awakened and was in the presence of the divine. He was listening to this beautiful singing and music and a Lady appeared. The words in the original Indian narrative are fascinating. He saw a Lady who was so beautiful she radiated like the sun and she spoke to him in the most tender way. She called him "My dearest Juan"—"Juanito," which means "one who is closest to me." She introduced herself by saying, "I am the mother of the true God through whom one lives." Then she told him to tell the bishop that the mother of the true God through whom one lives wanted the bishop to build a temple here at Tepeyac hill. So Juan went excitedly to the bishop with the good news of this beautiful vision. But when he tried to see the bishop he got the run-around. Finally he saw the bishop and told him the story. The bishop listened to him but was indifferent. So he returned feeling very rejected because he had failed the Lady. Then comes one of the most beautiful parts of the narrative. Feeling inferior and unworthy he went back to the Lady and said, "You know, the bishop didn't listen to me. I am just a poor Indian. I am nothing. I am worse than a bunch of dried-up worms or broken sticks. I am nobody. Send somebody who is important, somebody who is well known and respectable." But the Lady told him, "My son, I have many messengers whom I could pick. I have many ambassadors whom I could choose. But it is in every way precise that you, the smallest of my children, be my messenger to the bishop. I want you to go."

So he went back and this time the bishop listened a bit more and asked him for a sign. The bishop was surprised when the Indian did not hesitate. He said, "Of course I will bring you the sign." So he ran back and told the Lady, who said, "Come back tomorrow and I will give you the sign." So he went home, and when he arrived he found that his uncle was sick and dying. He decided that he would get a priest to come and anoint his uncle in the last rites before going to the Lady. Here it almost becomes a comedy. He went around the other side of the hill so the Lady would not stop him. He had to get to the bishop and so he went around the other side of the hill. To his amazement the Lady stopped him. He was embarrassed and apologetic and said, "I really was not running out on you but I have to get a priest for my uncle." The Lady assured him that his uncle was well and that he was to go up and get the sign which was waiting for him. So he went up to the top of the barren hill and there he found the most beautiful roses. He cut the roses and put them in his tilma and took them to the bishop. And the bishop finally saw them. When the flowers fell to the ground the image appeared on the tilma for the bishop and everyone to see. The image has been on the tilma from 1531 to the present day.

The most sophisticated scientific commissions have studied the tilma and their conclusion is that, by the most scientific standards, the image should not exist. But it is there. They said that the paint has never penetrated the cloth and therefore it should have crumbled away. And the cloth is a type that normally disintegrates in ten to twenty years. Nevertheless, it is still there after more than 450 years. There are no brush marks or finger marks on the painting. If it was painted, the paint would have had to be thrown at it. There have been several scientific commissions, the latest one from NASA, all concluding that there is no scientific explanation.

But what happened to the people is actually more important than what happened at that moment. The people who had wanted to die now wanted to live. The people who had wanted to have nothing to do with the missionaries now began to come and ask for instruction so they could be baptized. The people who had only lamented now began to sing and dance and make pilgrimages that continue to this day. What happened that brought them from wanting to die to wanting to live? What happened that brought them from not wanting to listen to the missionaries to coming and asking for instruction so they could become a part of this new church? During the next ten years there were more than eight million baptisms recorded. The people wanted to come. I do not know exactly what happened but it demands that we seek an explanation. As long as we try to understand through categories of western thought—as long as we try to impose western mariological, devotional categories—we will never understand the power of God's intervention through Tepeyac. The Lady did not appear to a westerner; she appeared to a native American. She did not speak a western language. She spoke a native American language.

What is the meaning of Guadalupe? When Juan Diego was walking to church, he heard beautiful music. He heard such beautiful singing that he thought he had died and gone to heaven. At the end of the story he presented the sign to the bishop, and the sign was flowers—flowers more beautiful than anyone had ever seen. In the Indian understanding this divine revelation took place in the context of music and flowers. For the Indian world, the main category for the divine was the beautiful. You did not speak about God in rational terms. You spoke about God in terms of beauty, in terms that were only suggestive because God is God. God is beyond all of my categories. And so we cannot corral God into a dictionary definition or the definition of a theological dogma. God is God and therefore God is greater than my expressions of God. Only in the power of music and flowers can we communicate the divine. The Guadalupe story begins with the sign of music and ends with the sign of flowers. Therefore, for the Indian world, they are no longer just human. Divinity is erupting and speaking to them in a way they can understand.

Secondly, the Lady appears at Tepeyac. Tepeyac had been the most sacred site of the Indian mother goddess, the earth goddess. It had been the site of pilgrimages from far-away lands from time immemorial. Different tribes came to venerate the sanctuary of the earth goddess, who had her sanctuary at Tepeyac. It was the custom of the Spaniards to rename every sacred site of the Indians, and they had renamed this site Guadalupe because there is a shrine of Guadalupe in Spain. Our Lady of Guadalupe in Spain had been the patroness of the reconquest of Spain against the Arabs, and then she had been the patroness of Cortez who came to the Americas. It was at Tepeyac, the famous shrine of the mother goddess, that the Lady appeared and told him, "I am the mother of the true God, through whom one lives."

The true God was the Spanish understanding of God but the term was incomprehensible to the Indian world. For them the imagery of God was the one through whom one lives. For the Indian world, nothing would exist if God took power away from it. We exist only because God sustains our existence. Therefore their term for God was "the one through whom one lives." The Spanish concept of God was incomprehensible to the Indians and the Indian concept of God was abominable to the Spaniards. The Lady united the Spanish concept with the Indian concept in one image of God. She began to unite what appeared to be two irreconcilable religions. She began a profound incarnation of the gospel.

The mother of the true God through whom one lives radiates divinity. She radiates the sun and begins to usher in the maternal, the female, aspect of the deity. For the Indian world a god that was exclusively male was incomprehensible. A god that was exclusively male could not be a god because it would be incomplete. The God that the European Christians presented was strongly and exclusively a male God. For the Indian world there was always the Father God who acted and the Mother God who asked. And the two always acted in concert. The Mother asked and the Father gave, but the Father would not give what the Mother would not ask for. In the message of Guadalupe you have the Mother who listens to her children to remedy all their miseries, their pain and suffering. The Mother is listening so that she might present, and when the Mother presents the Father cannot deny. It is a powerful duality that is understood by the simple people. When you ask many of our people, "Why is devotion to Mary so important to you?" they will respond, "Oh, Father, the church is so complicated. The Mother is so simple."

I have been pastor of a downtown parish for five years. It is a great sanctuary of poor people coming to pray. I have learned more about the imagery of God and about prayer from them than I had ever learned before. It is true when Jesus, in the gospels of Mark and Matthew, praises the Father because what is hidden from the wise and the intelligent has been revealed to the little ones. This is the mother in the gospel of John who, with her mother's intuition, notices that they are running out of wine and presents it to Jesus because she knows Jesus will act.

This is the true mother of the God through whom one lives and her greatest gift is her son. In the Guadalupe image Mary is not carrying a child. You do not see the child in the Guadalupe image but it is there. If you look at it very carefully, right over the womb of Guadalupe you will see the Indian symbol for the center of the universe. Guadalupe presents herself with a black band around her waist which is a sign of maternity—a sign that she is carrying a child. You will also see that her cheeks are the cheeks of a woman in about the third month of pregnancy. They retain a lot of water. Guadalupe appears with a Christ child in her womb because the greatest gift she will give will be the new center of the universe, the new center of our life, which is Christ the Lord. So she is a perfectly christocentric presentation of a new beginning that will listen to the people and be among them to help and to guide them.

But this Lady who is the mother of the true God through whom one lives, this Lady who appears as the divine revelation, is herself not a goddess. For the Indian world the gods were always beyond our power to know. Therefore they always wore a mask and had no eyes to see. In Guadalupe a beautiful face appears that not only can be seen but has eyes that see you and me. When you study the eye of Guadalupe under a microscope you see the figure of a person in that eye. That figure is not Juan Diego as many feel that it is. In 1531 it was Juan Diego but at this moment the power of Guadalupe is that everyone who looks on her in faith sees himself or herself reflected in an accepting way in her eye. The image of the human person in Guadalupe's eye is the image of you and of me. Generations of people have seen themselves accepted by the mother of the true God through whom one lives. That is the power of Guadalupe to lift up the downtrodden, to give them a new dignity, a new self-appreciation, and to move them forward. It is this Lady who picks the Indian, the one whom the world says has nothing to offer, the one whom the world says is a minor. And she tells the Indian, "You are to be my most trusted messenger." She sends the Indian to tell the bishop what to do and eventually the bishop obeys.

Liberation theology did not begin with Gustavo Gutierrez. Liberation theology began with Our Lady of Guadalupe and

Juan Diego. She spoke to the one whom the world had stepped on and put down and said, "It is you who are to speak in my name. It is you who are to bring about the new temple." For the Indian world the new temple was not a new church building but a complete way of life in which there would be compassion, understanding, and justice.

The result of Guadalupe has been the beginning of a new people. But the full result is not yet accomplished. The full result of Jesus of Nazareth is not yet accomplished. Jesus brought redemption, but we still have sin in the world, we still have oppression, and we still have suffering. Guadalupe started something new. Guadalupe initiated a new understanding of God, a new understanding of God's greatest gift, Jesus. But it also initiated a new understanding of God as Mother and Father God. This new image of the people begins the fourfold liberation of the Mexican people, the Latin American people.

First is the political and economic liberation. No major move for independence or justice in Mexico or Latin America has started that was not under the banner of Our Lady of Guadalupe. Mexican independence began with an ex-seminary rector who called together all the ex-seminarians to become the army of independence. They fought under the banner of Our Lady of Guadalupe. More than fifty percent of the line officers of the Mexican army of independence were ordained priests. That tradition of church and politics is not understood by Rome or the United States or Latin America today. It was Cura Morelos who was the first lieutenant at Cura Largo. The father of Mexico was an excommunicated priest but the banner was the banner of Our Lady of Guadalupe. When Zapata started the movement to return the land to the people, there was Our Lady of Guadalupe. And Our Lady of Guadalupe was the banner that pulled Cesar Chavez and the people together. There is no greater power than the power of the symbol that pulls people together and gives them the power to work and struggle together for a common cause.

Our Lady started the liberation from sexual oppression because in Guadalupe violated womanhood finds a new dignity. Guadalupe was unsoiled by the hands that had soiled the women, and through her the Mexican women began to find a new dignity. Even though the world might prostitute poor women and men might suffer castration, God can virginize and give potency to that which the world prostitutes and makes impotent. Guadalupe responds to the pain and the agony and the shame of violated womanhood and violated manhood and restores and begins to give a new sense of self-worth to that which the world has condemned as worthless.

Guadalupe is the beginning of a social and psychological liberation because in Juan Diego she gives to the downtrodden a new sense of dignity. As God called the people out of Egypt to be a new people, as God made Jesus of Nazareth, who had nothing in the eyes of the world, to be the Son of God and the savior, so God continues to call the poor and the oppressed of the world to be the messengers of the gospel. Pope Paul VI said beautifully that the sign of the kingdom is that the poor themselves begin to proclaim the kingdom and take it to others. It is not the rich and the powerful of the world who evangelize the poor, but it is the poor and the oppressed and the downtrodden of the world who experience the love of God and turn to the kingdom and then offer something new to the rest of the world. The poor who are convinced by the world that they are nobody find that they are somebody in God's eyes. They begin to throw away their "nobodyness" and walk upright and offer something new to the world. It began with Juan Diego, and that beginning continues today with people in the barrios, people in the basic Christian communities, people whose material poverty is no longer an obstacle to their spiritual richness.

Guadalupe is the beginning of religious liberation. The people took in the religion of the missionaries and combined it with their own religion. Throughout the world when the gospel is brought by missionaries and the people receive it according to what they have, together they produce something new. In Guadalupe the beautiful statement, "I am the true mother, the mother of the true God through whom one lives," begins a new religious expression. It will truly be Christian because it has received the word of the gospel. It will truly be indigenous American because that word of the gospel is now producing something new that is authentically Christian but not necessarily European Christian or North American Christian or western

Christian. It is truly the birth of a new people of God with new imagery, new religious experiences, new forms of piety and social morality. It will be truly evangelical. It will not force the people to cease being who they are as a people in order to become Christians.

Guadalupe begins the true incarnation of the liberating and empowering message of Jesus in the Americas. As Hellenistic Christianity once opened the doors for the gospel to go into new areas of the world that it had not yet touched, Guadalupe Christianity today opens the possibility for new understandings of God—for understanding the feminity of God and for understanding the treasure the peoples contribute to make Christianity more faithful to the gospel and to the people. The theological and ecclesial structures of the west have difficulty understanding this. This new church of the people is not in opposition to, but is a source of enrichment for, the total universal church. As we begin to go into the third millennium we will find in the ranks of the poor and the suffering, who have no strength and dignity except in their God and the mother of their God, new expressions of the gospel that will enrich all of us.

Today devotion to Our Lady of Guadalupe continues to grow, to be explored, and to be rediscovered. Our explanations do not make it powerful. It is powerful because it lives in the minds and hearts of the people. It is a fire that is pulling the people together in spite of all obstacles, and is offering them new imagery into universal Christianity that I believe will enrich and unite all the peoples of the third millennium. As Guadalupe was able to begin the unity of two irreconcilable religions into one new form of Christianity, that power will become even greater in the third millennium. Jesus prayed that we might all be one, not by killing anyone, nor destroying anyone, nor making anyone cease to be who they are. Jesus prayed that we might all be one by truly celebrating who we are—by uniting and harmonizing our differences. The differences will not be a source of division but will bring us closer and closer together. In Guadalupe the unity of the irreconcilable begins in the Americas, and in the third millennium it can come to fruition.

Mary and the People:
The Cult of Mary and Popular Belief

John R. Shinners, Jr.

Thirty-four years ago, the anthropologist Edward Banfield made a cultural study of a small southern Italian village. The people there, he found, venerated five local madonnas under five different names, attributing to each madonna a different purpose. He tells the story of how a young seminarian from the village attempted to explain to an old woman that there was in fact only *one* madonna. She laughed at him and said, "You have studied with the priests for eight years and you haven't even learned the differences between the madonnas!"[1]

With her remark, we enter the realm of popular religion, and Banfield's story is a classic example of the conflict between learned and popular culture, between official belief and lived belief, between theology and popular religion.[2] The members of learned culture address the existence and purpose of God through the methods of theology. The members of popular culture, on the other hand, address these same questions through the practices of popular religion. My purpose here is to move us away from Mary as she is understood by the members of learned culture and to consider instead the role she plays in popular culture.

Popular religion is a phrase that begs definition. By it I mean those religious beliefs and devotional practices cultivated by ordinary Christians. Several points, I would say, characterize it. First, it does not concern itself with theological nuance or ambivalence. In religious matters, it craves certainty. Religious faith is an assent to mystery which is always ineffable. Thus faith must play itself out between the poles of certainty and doubt. But popular religion eschews doubt. It tends to accept propositions about faith unhesitatingly and uncritically.

Second, popular religion seeks tangible proof of the presence of the divine and it seeks effective ways to tap divine power. As the historian Jacob Huizinga noted, among popular believers "religious ideas tend to crystallize into images."[3] Because of this tendency, popular religion is prone to rely on physical signs and wonders as proofs of the divine. Pilgrim shrines and the miracles that issue from them affirm both the reality and the presence of God and his saints. As Victor Turner puts it, pilgrim shrines represent a "tear in the veil" that separates heaven and earth.[4] God (or Mary) is there. A pilgrim at Lourdes, for example, remarks that "Lourdes is a corner of heaven; you feel you're no longer on earth."[5] Once the certainty of God's presence is established, adherents of popular religion seek ways to profitably engage God's divine power. Material objects (relics, rosaries dipped in Lourdes water, scapulars, images) are employed as conduits of divine power. Furthermore, the relationships that ordinary believers tend to establish with God and the saints are often contractual. In return for some form of payment (a vow of pilgrimage or self-mortification, a physical offering) God will bestow favors. As Robert Schreiter points out, among popular believers prayers of petition and prayers of thanksgiving for petitions granted tend to take precedence over general prayers of praise.[6]

Finally, popular religion is affective—it comes from the heart, is emotionally focused, and intensely human. With all these aspects of popular religion in mind, one could say that popular religion is marked by a literal-mindedness. (We shouldn't make the mistake of assuming that popular religion is the exclusive province of theologically unsophisticated lay people. Everyone, well educated or not, cleric or lay, needs to express religious belief in physical ways. And all believers, I would suggest, embrace some aspects of popular religion in their devotional life—whether they admit it or not.)

We see all of these characteristics of popular religion in the history of the popular cult of Mary. Throughout Christian history, the popular image of Mary has remained remarkably stable. People in almost all ages have been attracted to Marian devotion for similar reasons.

This paper explores four recurring popular images of Mary. In what follows I am only concerned with *images* of Mary —images that are not necessarily realities. What interests me as an historian of popular religion is what people *perceive* Mary to be; what Mary is primarily is a matter for theologians and biblical scholars to debate. Furthermore, I will focus primarily on the public manifestations of devotion to Mary—that is, those aspects of her cult that surface in Marian pilgrimages and festivals, in publicly acclaimed apparitions, and in sermons and stories meant to inspire devotion. Unfortunately, space is too short for me to explore devotions to Mary that individuals perform in private—the rosary, novenas, and so on.

Before I proceed to these images, it strikes me that a whirlwind historical tour of the popular cult of Mary is in order. It will help set the various circumstances within which these popular Marian images have worked themselves out.[7]

The beginnings of the cult are obscure, although a lot of scholarly energy has been spent trying to pinpoint them. A favorite pursuit has been the attempt either to locate the cultural antecedents of the cult or to define the psychological need which generates mother worship. Cultural anthropologists and historians rightly see aspects of the veneration of Mary as borrowings from pre-Christian earth-mother and fertility cults. Jungian psychologists locate the appeal of Mary in society's corporate need to express the archetypical feminine and maternal images of the collective unconscious. Freudians see in the cult a sublimation of male oedipal urges.[8] All of these theories fail for various reasons.

Whatever the misty origins of her cult, Mary very early became a figure for devotion among the Christian community. The earliest example of the artistic representation of Mary comes from a fresco of the virgin and child painted in about 150 A.D. in the catacomb of Priscilla in Rome, and an early fragmentary version of the prayer of petition to Mary, the *Sub tuum praesidium*, dates from the late third or early fourth century.[9] These early references aside, it is probably safe to say that the real impetus for the cult begins at the Council of Ephesus in 431, when—partly by virtue of the shrewd political maneuverings of Cyril of Alexandria—the dogmatic definition of Mary as theotokos (the bearer of Jesus both in his humanity and divinity) was declared.[10] Cyril's victory over his Nestorian opponents ensured the success of the cult of Mary because it underscored her unique role as the bearer of *God*. While church fathers and later theologians preferred the ambiguous term—in either Greek or Latin—"God-bearer" to "mother of God" (a title first officially used of Mary at the Second Vatican Council) it is easy to see how this fine distinction would be lost on ordinary people.

Ephesus, of course, was a thriving city of the eastern Roman empire. At the same time in the western empire, civilization was in decline as the Roman imperial administration collapsed and Germanic tribes overwhelmed the empire's borders. Marian devotions endured, as did the church, through the seven hundred years of social and economic disorder that we call the dark ages, but neither of them could be said to have prospered as religion retreated into the haven of monasteries.

The popular cult of Mary began its first vigorous stage of growth during the eleventh and twelfth centuries as European culture revived. A flourishing trade economy led to the rebirth of cities where soon, fed by the lucre of a new merchant class, glorious Gothic cathedrals (usually dedicated to Mary) and sophisticated schools of theology sprang up.

By the twelfth century, devotion to Mary was widespread.[11] Theological inquiry had produced a high christology which tended to distance Jesus from ordinary people. He, along with the awesome figure of his Father, was king and judge. Like the distant feudal kings whom ordinary people seldom encountered but whose justice was all too sure as royal bureaucracies burgeoned, Christ was much too powerful, much too threatening to be approached directly. It made much better sense to cultivate the attentions of his mother, who, like a kind-hearted feudal noblewoman, could bend her son's ear in one's favor. (Recall that the very names by which we commonly know Mary —Our Lady, Notre Dame, Madonna—are respectful titles given to feudal aristocrats. This feudal imagery dates from the eleventh and twelfth century.[12]) Churches were raised in her honor; her miracle-working shrines multiplied and became the goal of pilgrims; even her scarce relics abounded. Since Mary was believed to have been bodily assumed into heaven, no corporal relics of her were available as they were for other saints. But other bits and pieces associated with her turned up in astonishing numbers. Her maternity dress was enshrined at Chartres, her slipper at Soisson.[13] Marina Warner points out that strands of her hair were available throughout Europe in a variety of tints from blonde to black and, as she says, "in quantities that would have made a grizzly bear hirsute."[14] And if, as they say, there were enough pieces of the true cross available in the middle ages to build a boat, there was enough milk of the virgin to float it.[15]

The first challenge to the popular cult of Mary came with the reformation. While many Protestant theologians rejected her veneration on scriptural grounds, both Protestant and Catholic thinkers alike scorned the excesses of popular belief. "I desire that the cult of Mary be totally abandoned," wrote Martin Luther, "solely because of the abuses that arise from it."[16] But Erasmus, the great Catholic humanist, had been on the attack even before the separation of the church. His caustic barbs against distorted, superstitious Marian piety make for some of the wittiest reading from the age. His stance was clear: "No veneration of Mary is more beautiful," he wrote, "than the imitation of her humility."[17]

If anything, Protestant criticisms of the Marian cult increased Catholic enthusiasm for it. Catholics felt that Mary was being blasphemed; thus they multiplied their efforts to preserve her exalted status. (The same is true of eucharistic devotions, which were partly aimed at refuting the Protestant criticism of the doctrine of the real presence.)

Marian devotions reached a second peak in the seventeenth century, a hundred years after the reformation. The cult arrived at new heights of devotional excess, especially in France, a country torn first by Huguenot-Catholic divisions and then by the Jansensist controversy. In France we find new devotions to the virgin's left foot or to the sole of her shoe.[18] Confraternities of the "slaves of Mary" (imported from Italian practice) bound themselves in spiritual slavery to Mary, wearing small chains about their wrists or necks as signs of their bondage.[19] The "sanguinary vow" gained wide appeal. This was a vow to defend even to martyrdom the belief in the immaculate conception—which was not yet even official Catholic doctrine.[20] Popular manuals of devotion multiplied among an increasingly literate population. These manuals, often filled with most alarming and bizarre bits of pious humbug about Mary, fed the unquenchable popular thirst for Marian devotion.

All this came crumbling down with the eighteenth century enlightenment. Few of the *philosophes* had much use for what they saw to be the extravagant superstitions of religion, particularly the superstitions of authoritarian Catholicism. Led by the popular writings of Voltaire (a secular Erasmus in spirit) they dismissed the great Marian catalogue of miraculous interventions as gullible offenses against reason. Even the church, increasingly restrained by secular power and tempted by enlightenment rationalism, lost interest in promoting the cult. Marian feasts were stricken from local church calendars, shrines fell into ruin, excessive devotions were discouraged.[21] The disbanding of the Jesuits, always promoters of the cult, in 1783, threw even more water on the Marian fires. During the French Revolution, some churches removed their statues of Mary and replaced them with the goddess of reason—the final blow, so it seemed.

But the failure of the republican ideals of the Revolution and the conservative reaction which ensued, romanticism's rejection of the enlightenment program, and the Catholic revival under the heavy hand of the long-lived Pius IX signaled the rebirth of the Marian cult with a vengeance. The nineteenth century marked the beginning of the "Age of Mary," as some Catholic writers have called it. By mid-century, apparitions of

Mary were popping up all over Europe—especially in France. She appeared at Paris in 1830, Rome in 1842, La Salette in 1846, Lourdes in 1858, Croatia in 1865, Bohemia in 1866, Normandy in 1871, Knock in 1879. The dogmatic proclamation of the immaculate conception (*Ineffabilis Deus*) in 1854, issued in part because so many Catholics seemed to favor the idea, signaled the official rehabilitation of Mary.

The first sixty years of the twentieth century saw the continued importance of Marian enthusiasms. More apparitions—at Fatima in 1917, Beauraing, Belgium, in 1932 and again in Belgium at Banneaux the next year—suggest the frame of mind of the faithful. Marian confraternities blossomed like the flowers of May: Father Kolbe's Militia of the Immaculate Conception, founded on the heels of Fatima in 1917; Frank Duff's Legion of Mary, founded in 1921; the Blue Army, founded in 1947 and said to have fifteen million members by 1959.[22] The infallible doctrine of the assumption in 1950 marked another jewel in Mary's crown. This was a fitting accolade for most mariologists whose motto had become (in René Laurentin's words) *numquam satis*—never enough honor can be given to Mary.[23] The impetus of the Marian cult seemed unstoppable. The dogmatic definitions of Mary as mediatrix of all graces or as co-redemptress were the cherished goal of the Marianists at the Second Vatican Council. Of course, their hopes were dashed. The council's accommodation of Catholicism to the modern world, its re-emphasis on the scriptural foundations of faith, and its call to the social gospel seemed to have temporarily stanched the flow of Marian piety.[24] Or did it? Thousands made the pilgrimage to the unapproved shrine at Garabandal, Spain, where apparitions emerged daily between 1961 and 1965, and an estimated seven to eight million people have visited Medjugorje since 1981.[25]

With this history out of the way, let us turn to the images that have continually informed the cult of Mary. Mary is known by hundreds of names: Mother, Virgin, Queen, Immaculate Conception, Our Lady of Mercy, of Sorrows, of Peace, of Perpetual Help, of the Highway, of the Rosary, of Chartres, Lourdes, Fatima, Guadalupe, and so on and so on. Her images seem almost infinitely malleable, and every age tends to shape her according to its own desires. Nevertheless there are certain constants in her image. The following are four of the more important ones.

Throughout the history of her cult, Mary has been portrayed as a restorer of health, a healer. Unexpected, unrelenting, debilitating illness is one of the hardest burdens of the human condition, so it is hardly surprising that in all ages people have petitioned for divine help when the medical technologies of their day fail them. This search for divine healing is the most constant element of the popular veneration of the saints in general and Mary in particular. The thousands of shrines of Mary have been, and still are, places for seeking cures. During the long centuries of her cult, the number of miraculous cures attributed to her would number in the thousands.

It is a decidedly difficult task for an historian to assess the authenticity of miraculous cures. If we were to speak of a sociology of healing, then we could conclude that miracles come easier to an age—like the middle ages—whose medical knowledge is limited and whose sense of the immanence of the holy is more acute. We now know, for instance, that many illnesses are self-limiting; they cure themselves after a time. We also know much more about the psychogenic character of certain illnesses. Headaches and other forms of neuralgia, certain arthritic conditions and intestinal ailments, and certain skin diseases—eczema, for instance—often have psychological origins which would make them susceptible to faith healings. Ronald Finucane found that cures of precisely these types of conditions figure prominently in the miracles that are recorded at medieval shrines.[26] However, the understanding that such cures proceed from natural or psychological processes rather than supernatural interventions makes them no less miraculous to the people who are relieved of their suffering.

Today we hold modern claims of miraculous cures to a higher standard of proof. An air of skepticism—bred by the scientific standards of our age and enormous advances in medicine over the last fifty years—hangs over our assessment of modern cures. The attitude of French author Anatole France (whose book on Lourdes caused a national scandal at the turn of the century) is representative. Visiting the shrine at Lourdes and viewing the hundreds of crutches and canes left by pilgrims claiming miraculous cures there, he asked, "What? No wooden legs?"[27] But the claims of miraculous cures at Marian shrines still persist. There have been hundreds of cures claimed at Lourdes (the most famous curative Marian shrine) in the last hundred years, although only sixty-two have been certified by the church as miraculous. (Documentary evidence for some of these cures would leave even the most skeptical commentator speechless.[28])

In the popular imagination, Mary's second role—as an intercessor between heaven and earth, a mediatrix—is equally as powerful as her role as healer. This idea of the intercession of saints on behalf of the living members of the church on earth is of course an old one. It probably draws inspiration from the Roman notion of patronage—patrons being those powerful individuals who intervene with a higher authority on behalf of their weaker clients.[29] But in the Marian cult, patronage takes on even greater force. In the popular eye Mary not only pleads before God on behalf of her human clients, she actually influences his judgments owing to her position as his mother. Mary becomes not just a patroness or intercessor; she assumes the more powerful role of mediatrix—one who sways the decisions of the highest judge.

This idea, Greek in origin, was popular in the west by the ninth century. It appears clearly in the story of the clerk Theophilus, which was the inspiration for the Faust legend. The story originated in the eastern church in the fifth century, and was translated into Latin for western audiences by Paul the deacon, an academic in the court of Charlemagne, in the ninth century. Paul's translation, in fact, contains the first use of the Latin word "mediatrix" to refer to Mary. The legend tells the story of Theophilus, a bureaucrat who is disappointed because he has not received a post he desired. He makes a pact with the devil, pledging his soul in return for earthly success. In the end, however, he repents and prays to Mary to seek God's pardon of him. She intervenes and forces the devil to tear up Theophilus' contract.[30]

Mary's role as mediatrix became enormously popular in the west by the eleventh and twelfth centuries, both in theological discussions and in popular practice. By the twelfth century Mary's maternal mediation with Jesus is commonplace. The English monk Eadmer, a protégé of Anselm of Canterbury, wrote, "Sometimes salvation is quicker if we remember Mary's name than if we invoke the name of the Lord Jesus." Eadmer reasoned that Jesus "is the Lord and Judge of all men, discerning the merits of the individuals; hence he does not at once answer anyone who invokes him, but does so only after just judgment. But if we invoke the name of his Mother, her merits intercede so that he is answered even if the merits of him who invokes her do not deserve it."[31] The French historian and theologian Guibert of Nogent believed that Jesus obeys the desires of his mother because he abides by the fourth commandment. "As a good son in this world so respects his mother's authority that she commands rather than asks," he wrote, "so Christ, who undoubtedly was once subject to her, cannot, I am sure, refuse her anything; and what she demands, not by asking but by commanding, will surely come to pass."[32] Christ, in this imagery, becomes the young king—unmerciful and unimaginative—who plays it strictly by the rules, dispensing firm, untempered justice where it is due. But fortunately for us, he is tightly tied to his mother the queen's apron strings. We can mollify him, by pleasing his mother who, in return for our devotion, sways her son's judgments in our favor.

This completely unorthodox notion becomes the cornerstone for an extraordinary number of stories of the miracles of Mary. These collections, assembled in many places throughout the twelfth century, spread widely over Europe, carried on the lips of itinerant preachers and gathered in sermon manuals and devotional works.[33]

In these stories, Mary becomes the mother of mercy par excellence (an important Marian title, incidentally, probably introduced in the monasteries attached to Cluny in the tenth century).[34] She unhesitatingly intervenes to ensure the salvation of even the most depraved members of society, so long as they show some small devotion to her. Stories abound of murderers, robbers, thieves, and other social deviates who, hell-bound at death because of their grave sins, are spared at the eleventh hour by Mary's intervention. A daily "Hail Mary" on their part was enough to gain this intercession.[35]

The best known story in this genre concerns the thief Eppo. Let me relate it to you in a fifteenth-century version by the preacher Johannes Herolt:

> There once was a very great robber, a most wicked man, who thought of nothing but the service of the devil. Yet he had this good in him: he scrupulously fasted on bread and water during the vigil of the Blessed Mary; and, when he went out to rob he used to salute her with such devotion as he could, asking her not to allow him to die in mortal sin. But, being caught and brought to the gallows, he hung for three days and could not die. [Some versions add that he had a smile on his face the whole time, which surely must have riled the hangman.] And when he called to those passing by and asked them to bring a priest, one came with the judge and the people and he was taken down from the gallows. Then he said that it was the Blessed Virgin who kept him alive; and so he was set free, and afterwards he finished his life in a praiseworthy fashion.[36]

A version of the story from the thirteenth century provides us with the payoff that Herolt omits. Mary saved Eppo by holding him up by the feet while he hung for the three days![37]

I should add that in most medieval versions of the story of "the sinner saved by Mary," sinners are expected to perform penance for their faults before they are saved. Often they are returned from the dead for a few days to accomplish this. Usually no one gets off scot-free in these stories. Nevertheless, Mary often appears to be ethically blind. In one story she saves an abbess who is pregnant by intervening and removing the unborn child to the care of a hermit. The pregnant abbess thereby escapes ecclesiastical censure, but the nuns in her care who rightly denounced her to her bishop are expelled from the convent.[38] Too often in these stories, Mary emerges as a capricious judge who barters salvation to her devotees in exchange for a few cursory "Hail Mary's." This message threatens to make Christian faith, for the ordinary believer, seem little more than a convenient contractual arrangement, a sort of spiritual quid pro quo.

There is another obvious danger implicit in this image of Mary's role as intercessor and mediatrix. If it is taken to extremes, and it often has been, she threatens to become a second redeemer. This urge has been strong in Catholicism. It was at its worst from the time of the counter-reformation until the early twentieth century, the heyday of "mariolotry." For instance, one of the greatest eighteenth century devotees of Mary, St. Alphonse Liguori, approved the opinion of an earlier author who wrote: "If God is angry with a sinner and Mary takes him under her protection, she withholds the avenging arm of her Son, and saves him."[39] Another extreme example of Mary's redemptive powers comes from the seventeenth century when some French Catholics believed that it sufficed to be devoted to Mary alone in order to be saved.[40] A medieval story shows us how devotional balance could be maintained: "A clerk, trusting more in the mother than in the son, never stopped repeating the 'Hail Mary' as his only prayer. Once as he said the 'Hail Mary,' the Lord appeared to him, and said: 'My Mother thanks you much for all the salutations that you make to her; but still you should not forget to salute me also.' "[41]

Another devotional hazard is present in Mary's intercessory image. In the popular eye, she is often enough as prone to vengeance as her son. This especially happens when people doubt her power, and is a frequent motif in medieval stories. For instance, a man who doubted the authenticity of her slipper at Soisson found that his tongue shriveled up.[42] At the shrine of Genazzano, which emerged in the fifteenth century, a man doubted the virgin's miracles. Mary appeared to him and told him she would prove her power. He returned home to find his young son, healthy when his father left him, dying. Only when he returned with his son to the shrine did Mary heal the boy.[43]

Mary's tendency toward vengeance is still with us. At Medjugorje, the apparition informed the children that she was dis-
pleased that the local bishop had not approved the authenticity
of her appearances there. She warned him to be converted
"before it was too late." "I send him final warning," she said.
"Unless he is converted, my verdict and that of my Son Jesus
Christ will be upon him."[44] These spiteful images of Mary are
surely unworthy of her, but in the popular eye they confirm her
power and the trust we should put in it.

A third popular image of Mary regards her as a social critic
or prophetess. In this guise Mary's actions serve either as implicit criticisms of the social order or as prophetic political
reproaches to a world gone bad. This image appears rather
subtly in stories prior to the nineteenth century when it becomes much more overt. A thirteenth century story tells of a
rich nobleman and a poor widow both on their death beds. The
avaricious pastor of the parish hastened off to console the rich
lord and found him lying in his palace, clad in silk, lying on soft
cushions. Meanwhile, a messenger arrived asking the priest to
visit the dying widow. His deacon urged him to go. "What a
madman's idea," replied the priest, "to leave a noble patron for
a humble widow." The deacon asked if he could take the viati-
cum to the poor widow. The priest said yes and sent him on his
way. Arriving at the widow's poor hovel, he found her lying on
the hard ground, covered with straw. But around her knelt
Mary with a band of virgins. Mary attended to her, wiping the
sweat from her face. The deacon administered the eucharist to
the dying woman and saw to her final needs while Mary and the
virgins bowed down in reverence to the host. Then the deacon
hastened back to the nobleman's palace where he found the
dying man surrounded by black cats. A black devil plunged a
hook into the rich man's throat and carried his soul to hell.
Here, of course, we see a medieval version of the preferential
option for the poor played out.[45]

Mary's political criticisms become more frequent after the
French Revolution—the event which marks the ultimate secu-
larization of the political order. During the Revolution, for
instance, a tree holding a statue of Mary bled when revolution-

aries chopped it down. Reports circulated of men killed or maimed when they tried to take down statues and images of Mary.[46]

In the twentieth century, the popular religious imagination has made Mary an outspoken critic of communism. Sister Lucia, one of the visionaries at Fatima, revealed—somewhat belatedly—that Mary had called for prayers for the conversion of Russia. Mary Ann Van Hoof (whose bizarre Marian visions at Necedeh, Wisconsin, still draw a pilgrim following almost forty years after they began and four years after Van Hoof's death) pictured Mary as a sort of divine Joe McCarthy, sniffing out "commies" from on high. In an apparition attended by maybe 100,000 people on the Van Hoof farm on the feast of the Assumption, 1950, Mary reported: "The black clouds [of communism] are coming over, not to Europe, Asia, Australia, Africa, but to America—South and North America. Alaska is the first stepping stone. Remember the Pacific Coast!"[47] Later Mary began pinpointing the presence of Soviet submarines (she colloquially called them "subs") off the coast of Havana and at other strategic checkpoints.[48] Van Hoof's so-called revelations were mimicked by Veronica Leuken at Bayside, New York, in the 1970s and 1980s. An advertisement promoting Leuken's visions in 1984 reports this message: "Do not take lightly the reports of ships out on the sea and submarines. They are there, my child and my children, and they are not out for a joy ride. It is part of the master plan for the takeover of the United States and Canada."[49] A Catholic writing in the 1940s sums up Mary's role in the cold war: "Against Satan and his red threats, we have Mary."[50] It will be interesting to note what happens to Mary's politics in the era of *glastnost*.

The Mary who appears in these apparitions of the nineteenth and twentieth centuries is politically conservative. This should come as no surprise. European and North American popular religion tends to be zealously concerned with guarding tradition. The social and ideological changes promised by the modern world—whether they encompass such things as science, liberalism, socialism, and biblical criticism (all condemned by Pius IX in the Syllabus of Errors of 1864) or whether they be such things as communism, Vatican II, and the new liturgy—threaten the world view of those Catholics who believe in the enduring and eternal ways. (In contrast to the politically conservative Marian images of Europeans and Americans, Latin American popular religion sometimes, but not always, uses Mary for more liberal political ends.)

Mary's ultimate political criticisms are most obvious when she announces the apocalypse—something she has regularly done since La Salette. The apparition at La Salette in 1846 occurred in the midst of economic chaos as a severe famine gripped France. It warned that unless the people reformed their impious ways, the famine would endure, the potato crops would rot, wheat would turn to dust, young children would die of fever, and the wine grapes would perish.[51]

At Fatima the message passed on by Lucia from Mary was overtly apocalyptic. Later in her life, Lucia reported that at Fatima Mary told her that an aurora borealis that appeared over Europe in January 1938 was a sign that God was "about to punish the world for its crimes, by means of war, famine, and persecutions of the Church and of the Holy Father."[52] And of course the famous unrevealed "third secret of Fatima"—the one that according to legend makes popes' faces go ashen when they read it—has popularly been believed to predict the end of the world.

These apocalyptic warnings continue in the apparitions of the last decades. Veronica Leuken's visions at Bayside are explicitly apocalyptic with many implied visions of nuclear holocaust. Mary tells Veronica: "The hourglass is now almost empty. Days can be counted by hours."[53] In appropriately ominous nuclear imagery, she reports that "the Warning is coming upon mankind. There will be a tremendous explosion and the sky shall roll back like a scroll." Veronica then sees a red fireball rolling across the sky.[54] Likewise, the Mary of the visionaries at Medjugorje preaches the apocalypse. A letter to the pope by one of the children's advocates—a Franciscan priest—gives this message from Mary to the children: "The ninth and tenth secrets [given to the children] are grave. They are a chastisement for the sins of the world. The punishment is inevitable because we must not expect a conversion of the entire world. The chastisement can be decreased by prayers and penance, but it cannot be suppressed."[55] Allegedly she told the children that she appears so frequently at Medjugorje (every day for the last seven years) because this is her last appearance on earth.

Such prophecies are politically conservative. Usually when people feel compelled to predict the end of the world, what they really mean is that *their* world—the world in which they feel comfortable—has already ended. Harried by the insecurity and uncertainty they feel when faced with a changing world, they explicitly criticize that world by predicting its end. People do not predict the demise of a world that satisfies them. (From a liberal political perspective, I would argue that people living under oppression tend to see not the end of the world, but the coming of a utopia. This would be my interpretation of Fr. Virgil Elizondo's remarks about the liberating influence of Guadalupe in the new world.[56])

Such messages are as much about the visionaries' perceptions of their society as they are about anything specifically religious. Millennial prophecies are reproofs against the existing social order. That order has either swept away or radically altered cherished institutions and customs, or it is corrupt and oppressive and therefore must be replaced by a just society, a utopia. Modern Marian apparitions consistently see existing society as corrupted by change. They wax nostalgic for the stability, comfort, and predictability of tradition—especially Catholic tradition. The apparition at Bayside demands a return to the Latin mass; at Medjugorje, the apparition blames the evil of the world on Satan. "He destroys marriages, creates divisions between priests, obsessions, murders," it tells the children. "You should protect yourself from these things by fasting and prayer, especially by community prayer. Carry with you blessed objects; keep them in your houses." "Come back to the custom of holy water," Mary urges.[57] Come back, in short, to tradition. Veronica Leuken's visions say this: "My Son's Church has been laid out and the course to heaven, the way to Heaven has been given by Him. Therefore, change causes confusion and error. When you have something beautiful, when you have a firm foundation, you don't start boring holes in it, or you will weaken it."[58] Another of Leuken's apparitions—this one of Jesus in 1986—makes the point explicitly: "Satan entered by the Church upon earth. He . . . sat in on Vatican II and maneuvered all the outsiders to come in and distort my doctrines and distort the truth."[59] Here is what might be called pious nostalgia.

The final popular image of Mary I wish to explore is the image that highlights her historical reality—her image as woman. Mary blends together the roles of mother, comforter, nurturer, counselor, and friend—roles in which western culture traditionally casts women. This image, which gathers together aspects from the other images, is the most enduring, the most emotionally-charged image of Mary. What is most interesting about it is the way it intensely humanizes Mary in the eyes of believers. Mary's feminine aspect is what makes her so easily approachable. For example, William Christian tells how women in a modern Spanish village will often say, "Let's pay a call on the Virgin today," as if they were visiting a friend.[60] And in fact, she does the sort of things for people that friends do for friends, or mothers do for their children. One medieval miracle has her stand in for a nun who abandoned her convent for seventeen years. In another, a knight on his way to a tournament stops to pray at her chapel; he arrives late at the tournament only to find that he has won it. Mary wore his armor and jousted for him.[61]

People can establish such an intimate rapport with her that sometimes her universality becomes obscured. In the sixteenth century, St. Thomas More, in one of his religious dialogues, describes two women arguing over the relative merits of Our Lady of Walsingham (the most famous medieval English Marian shrine) and Our Lady of Ipswich. "Of all Our Ladies," says one woman, "I love best Our Lady of Walsingham."[62] Even today, when priests give penances of a certain number of "Hail Mary's" to confessing pilgrims at Fatima, the pilgrims—familiar with so many Mary's—often ask, "To which Blessed Virgin should I pray?"[63]

In the popular eye Mary is the perfect friend and mother,

for not only is she endowed with every laudable human quality, she is also the all powerful queen of heaven. Paradoxically she blends perfect humanity and divinity together (but then so does her son). She traffics easily back and forth between heaven and earth, but her human aspect always ensures us that she will be approachable. What better advocate could one ask?

Finally, we must ask whether the church hierarchy can effectively control popular Marian devotions. To an extent it can. It can do so by channeling them toward more legitimate forms of piety. Two examples come to mind. The first is at Lourdes. Almost as soon as the shrine was officially approved, the ceremonies there took on a christocentric focus. Daily masses are said at several sites on the grounds of the shrine, and one of the most important events of the ritual there is the afternoon procession of the Blessed Sacrament. Significantly, as many cures are reported during this procession as at the miraculous baths themselves.[64] Since Vatican II, the anointing of the sick is administered daily to the infirm, highlighting the sacramental focus of the devotion.[65]

A more interesting example of the effective church control of a Marian cult is the case of the shift in devotions at the Shrine of Our Lady of Mount Carmel in East Harlem, New York City. Three years ago Robert Orsi undertook a sociological study of this cult and its importance to newly-immigrated southern Italians who settled in East Harlem.[66]

The cult, which began in 1882, centered on a statue of the madonna imported from Italy and set up in the Church of Our Lady of Mount Carmel. The main activity of the cult was a two-week-long celebration or *festa* of eating and drinking in mid-July which culminated in a formal procession to the statue in the church. In its heyday, the procession drew thousands of Italian-Americans from miles around.

By any definition the early devotions surrounding this festival were excessive. At the end of each procession there was a band of penitents walking barefoot or crawling on their knees over the hot July asphalt. These people had vowed this penance to Mary in exchange for some favor bestowed by her. Until the practice was forbidden in 1920, women would be dragged down the aisle of the church licking the floor as they went. Other devout pilgrims licked the steps leading into the church.[67]

A strong dose of magical religion surrounded the devotion. Following a very ancient practice, pilgrims left *ex voto* offerings at the shrine in payment for blessings and miracles bestowed. These *ex votos* were wax models of healed limbs and organs or heavy wax candles commensurate in weight to the favor granted. Scapulars of Our Lady of Mount Carmel blessed at the shrine were believed to ward off all danger—even to deflect bullets![68]

But gradually these excesses were channeled or curtailed as the official church exerted greater control over the festa. In 1904 the statue of the madonna was crowned—a formal, Vatican-approved ceremony which elevates a Marian shrine to the status of a sanctuary, and also gives the church greater leverage over popular devotion.[69] By the 1950s what had begun as a festa centered on a statue that happened to be in a particular church had now become a festa sponsored by that church. A message to the parish from the pastor of Mount Carmel in 1953 underscores the change in the cult orchestrated by the priests of the parish. "The Mount Carmel feast," he wrote, "is not a feast of games, orgies, and outside pastimes. Although there will be some moderate outside signs of joy, yet the Mount Carmel feast, the real and true feast, will be in the church, at the feet of the miraculous statue of the Virgin, it will be in your hearts."[70] As the clergy took greater control of the feast, the miracles attributed to the madonna diminished. Today hundreds of letters are still received at the shrine, but they come mostly from elderly Italian-Americans who still cling to the old ways. These letters, often in Italian and directly addressed to the madonna, reflect the touching piety of simple believers. "I have need of many graces and I have great faith in the madonna," one petitioner writes. "I am eighty-six years old and I used to come to the festa as often as I could. But now I am very old; I can't leave the house; I have great need of the madonna." Another letter is more direct: "I can no longer come to the festa because of my age; hold me under your cloak [the ancient devotion to Mary's cloak of mercy] and bless me."[71]

The history of popular devotion to Mary shows that the concern that veneration to her will become excessive if not carefully checked is warranted. These excesses are bred not only by the thirst that ordinary people have for tangible signs of the existence of the divine and its immanence on earth. They have also been bred in part by a clergy who were, until relatively recently, ill-equipped through their lack of education to direct the devotions of the laity to more approved forms of piety, or too swayed by an absolutist and triumphalist church which encouraged such dependence on signs and wonders as a bulwark against the rationalist and liberal challenges of the modern age. Things seem to have changed now, largely due to the reforms and theological repositionings of the Second Council. But have they really changed?

Andrew Greeley, in a rather eccentric book on Mary written in 1977, uttered this manifesto: "[T]he popular Mariology [which] seems bent on multiplying titles and miracles (where it survives at all) . . . is likely to turn off both Catholics and non-Catholics. I will confess," he continued, "to being most impatient with popular Mariology even in its present moribund state. It is creepy, and does a great disservice to Our Lady, who has been the prisoner of creeps far too long."[72]

Strong words these—words that show no appreciation for the impulses that drive popular religion. Any theological reshaping of the image of Mary will have to take account of these popular impulses. For in every age Mary's image tells us as much about ourselves as it does about Mary.

If we divinize Mary (as liberation theologians seem prone to do), then we risk the abuses of mariolotry that have for so long cluttered her cult, the abuses that make her "creepy" for Greeley—and for many others as well. And of course we do a disservice to Mary. As John XXIII once remarked: "The Madonna is not pleased when she is put above her Son."[73] On the other hand, if we approach the other extreme, if we over-humanize the cult, we will satisfy those members of the learned tradition who find today that the cult rests on an unsure theological and historical footing. But this intensely human image of Mary—this Mary of history—will not satisfy the needs of everyday, affective piety, needs that demand a Mary who is a heavenly healer, intercessor, prophet, comforter, and friend. What theologians ignore, ordinary people will provide: Lourdes and Fatimas—and even Medjugorjes—will probably always be with us.

Notes

1. Edward C. Banfield, *The Moral Basis of a Backward Society* (New York, 1958), pp. 124–25.
2. Robert Redfield first elaborated this idea of a "great" and "little" cultural tradition in his study *Peasant Society and Culture* (Chicago, 1956), pp. 41–43.
3. Jacob Huizinga, *The Waning of the Middle Ages* (New York, 1954 [1949]), chapter 12.
4. Victor and Edith Turner, *Image and Pilgrimage in Christian Culture, Anthropological Perspectives* (New York, 1978), pp. 205–206.
5. René Laurentin, "The Persistence of Popular Religion," in *The Persistence of Religion,* Andrew Greeley and Gregory Baum, eds. (Concilium 81) (New York, 1973), p. 154.
6. In *Constructing Local Theologies* (Maryknoll, 1985), pp. 129–30. Schreiter's book is an excellent introduction to modern trends in the study of popular religion. See especially chapter 6.
7. For much of the cult's history which follows, I am indebted to Hilda Graef's excellent study, *Mary: A History of Doctrine and Devotion,* Vol. I, *From the Beginnings to the Eve of the Reformation* (New York, 1963) and Vol. II, *From the Reformation to the Present Day* (New York, 1965).
8. Michael Carroll surveys some recent approaches in his book, *The Cult of the Virgin Mary: Psychological Origins* (Princeton, 1986), chapter 2. His own Freudian explanation of the cult suffers both from psychological reductionism and from ahistorical generalizations. See also the

articles collected in *Mother Worship, Theme and Variation,* ed. James J. Preston (Chapel Hill, 1982).

9. Turner, *Image and Pilgrimage,* p. 150; Graef, *Mary,* v. I, p. 48.

10. Graef, *Mary,* v. I, pp. 101–111.

11. A recent interesting interpretation of the spread of the cult and the shifting artistic images of Mary is Penny Schine Gold's *The Lady and the Virgin, Image, Attitude, and Experience in Twelfth-Century France* (Chicago, 1985). The classic account of the medieval cult is Henry Adams' *Mont-Saint-Michel and Chartres* (New York, 1959 [1904]).

12. Bernard of Clairvaux, for instance, speaks of us as "servuli" (pages) who follow Our Lady (Graef, *Mary,* v. I, p. 24). A Franciscan preacher extensively develops this feudal imagery in a sermon from a fourteenth century sermon manual. See A.G. Little, *Studies in English Franciscan History* (Manchester, 1917), p. 149.

13. Benedicta Ward, *Miracles and the Medieval Mind. Theory, Record and Event, 1000–1215* (Philadelphia, 1982), pp. 142, 153–54.

14. Marina Warner, *Alone of All Her Sex, The Myth and the Cult of the Virgin Mary* (New York, 1976), p. 294.

15. Erasmus discusses the various relics of Mary's milk claimed throughout Europe in his dialogue "A Pilgrimage for Religion's Sake," in *The Colloquies of Erasmus,* trans. Craig R. Thomas (Chicago, 1965), pp. 295–96.

16. René Laurentin, *The Question of Mary,* trans. I.G. Pidoux (New York, 1965), p. 49.

17. Erasmus, *The Handbook of the Militant Christian,* trans. John P. Dolan (New York, 1964), p. 66.

18. Paul Hoffer, *La Devotion a Marie au Declin du XVIIe Siècle* (Paris, 1938), p. 114.

19. Graef, *Mary,* v. II, p. 34.

20. Ibid. p. 72.

21. Graef, *Mary,* v. II, pp. 77–78.

22. Laurentin, *The Question of Mary,* p. 10.

23. Ibid. p. 54.

24. See Gregory Baum, "Mary of the Magnificat," in *A Council*

for Peace, eds. Hans Küng and Jürgen Moltmann (Concilium) (Edinburgh, 1988), pp. xi–xiii.

25. Denis R. Janz, "Medjugorje's Miracles: Faith and the Profit," *Christian Century,* p. 724. The problem of the historical analysis of visions is enormously difficult. A good introduction to the topic is Karl Rahner's *Visions and Prophecies,* trans. Charles Henkey and Richard Strachen (New York, 1963). A fine example of historical interpretation is William A. Christian's *Apparitions in Late Medieval and Renaissance Spain* (Princeton, 1981).

26. Ronald C. Finucane, *Miracles and Pilgrims. Popular Belief in Medieval England* (Totowa, NJ, 1977), pp. 79–82.

27. Patrick Marnham, *Lourdes, A Modern Pilgrimage* (New York, 1981), p. 91.

28. Marnham gives a balanced discussion of these cures, ibid. chapter 8 and appendix III. See also Alan Neame, *The Happening at Lourdes: The Sociology of the Grotto* (New York, 1967).

29. See Peter Brown's brilliant book, *The Cult of Saints: Its Rise and Function in Latin Christianity* (Chicago, 1981).

30. For the background of the legend see Graef, *Mary,* v. I, p. 171. One version of the story can be found in Johannes Herolt's *Miracles of the Blessed Virgin Mary,* pp. 68–69 and comments, p. 139, n. 42. (See below, n. 32.)

31. Graef, *Mary,* v. I, p. 216.

32. Ibid. p. 205.

33. A fairly accessible translated selection of these stories is the fifteenth century *Miracles of the Blessed Virgin Mary* by Johannes Herolt, trans. C.C. Swinton Bland (London, 1928). Like most of the collections, it draws heavily on older material, in particular on the stories of the thirteenth century Dominican preacher Caesarius of Heisterbach. Other collections include *The Liber de Miraculis Sanctae Genetricis Mariae of Bernard of Pez,* Thomas Fr. Crane, ed. (Ithaca, 1925).

34. Graef, *Mary,* v. I, p. 203.

35. A succinct example: "A certain knight daily saluted the Blessed Virgin Mary, when he rose in the morning, and

when he lay down to sleep late in the day, with a 'Hail Mary' and never did any other good thing. And he was saved by the grace of the Virgin" (Herolt, *Miracles,* pp. 81–82).

36. Herolt, *Miracles,* pp. 22–23.
37. This from Etienne de Bourbon. See *Medieval Sermon Stories* in *Translations and Reprints from the Original Sources of European History,* Vol. III, No. 4 (revised) (Philadelphia, 1902).
38. Herolt, *Miracles,* pp. 42–43.
39. Graef, *Mary,* v. II, p. 75.
40. Ibid. p. 52.
41. Adams, *Mont-Saint-Michel and Chartres,* p. 289.
42. Ward, *Miracles and the Medieval Mind,* p. 143.
43. Anonymous, *The Virgin Mother of Good Counsel: A New Month of Mary* (Dublin, 1890).
44. Peter Hebblethwaite, "Medjugorje: A 'Pious Fraud,' " *National Catholic Reporter* 24 (No. 32, June 3, 1988), p. 9. (Review of Ivo Sivric's *La Face Cachee de Medjugorje.* Unfortunately, I was unable to consult this work.) For a less skeptical account of Medjugorje, see Svetozar Kraljevic's *The Apparitions of Our Lady at Medjugorje, 1981–1983. An Historical Account with Interviews,* ed. Michael Scanlon (Chicago, 1983).
45. Herolt, *Miracles,* pp. 86–89.
46. For a further review of the political images of Mary prevalent throughout the nineteenth century, see Thomas A. Kselman, *Miracles and Prophecies in Nineteenth-Century France* (New Brunswick, 1983), p. 209, n. 20.
47. Thomas A. Kselman and Steven Avella, "Marian Piety and the Cold War in the United States," *Catholic Historical Review* 62 (July 1986), p. 403.
48. Carroll, *The Cult of the Virgin Mary,* pp. 139–40.
49. Ibid. p. 139.
50. Warner, *Alone of All Her Sex,* p. 313.
51. Kselman, *Miracles and Prophecies,* pp. 62–63.
52. Lucia Santos (Sister Lucia of the Immaculate Heart), *Fatima in Lucia's Own Words: Sister Lucia's Memoirs,* ed. Louis Kondor (Fatima, 1976), p. 108.

53. Anonymous promotional letter from Our Lady of the Roses Shrine, Bayside, New York, mailed from San Luis Obispo, 17 July 1986, to a member of the Department of Religious Studies, Saint Mary's College, Notre Dame, p. 1.
54. Advertisement for the Bayside Shrine, *Toronto Star,* 17 March 1979, p. 67.
55. Quoted in the videotape, "Medjugorje: A Message of Peace for You. A Personal Account by Father Edward Serena," produced by the Center for Peace, Boston, 1985.
56. Virgil Elizondo, "Popular Religion as Support of Identity: A Pastoral-Psychological Case-Study Based on the Mexican American Experience in the USA," in *Popular Religion,* eds. Norbert Greinacher and Norbert Mette (Concilium) (Edinburgh, 1986).
57. "Medjugorje: A Message of Peace."
58. Advertisement for the Bayside Shrine, *Toronto Star,* 12 September 1981, p. H7.
59. Anonymous promotional letter from Our Lady of the Roses Shrine, p. 6.
60. William A. Christian, Jr., *Person and God in a Spanish Valley* (New York, 1972), p. 117.
61. Herolt, *Miracles,* pp. 43–45.
62. Thomas More, *A Dialogue Concerning Heresies* in *The Complete Works of St. Thomas More,* Thomas M.C. Lawler, Germain Marc'hadour and Richard C. Marius, eds. (Yale, 1981), Vol. 6, part 1, p. 99.
63. Karl Rahner, *Visions and Prophecies,* p. 34, n. 27.
64. Marnham, *Lourdes,* p. 114.
65. Ibid. pp. 104–05.
66. Robert Anthony Orsi, *The Madonna of 115th Street, Faith and Community in Italian East Harlem, 1880–1950* (Yale, 1985). Given its southern Italian origins, the cult has, not surprisingly, striking similarities to that festival described by Tullio Tentori in "An Italian Religious Feast: The *Fujenti* Rites of the Madonna dell'Arco, Naples," in *Mother Worship,* ed. James J. Preston (Chapel Hill, 1982).

67. Orsi, *The Madonna*, pp. xiii–xiv, 4.
68. Ibid. pp. 12, 67.
69. Ibid. p. 60.
70. Ibid. pp. 72–73.
71. Ibid. p. 252, n. 102.
72. Andrew Greeley, *The Mary Myth: On the Femininity of God* (New York, 1977), pp. 15–16.
73. Graef, *Mary*, v. I, epigraph.

Notes on the Contributors

ANNE CARR is Professor of Theology at the University of Chicago Divinity School. She is the author of *The Theological Method of Karl Rahner, Transforming Grace: Christian Tradition and Women's Experience* and *Search for Wisdom and Spirit: Thomas Merton's Theology of Self.*

DORIS DONNELLY, this book's editor, is an associate professor in the Department of Religious Studies at John Carroll University in University Heights, Ohio. She is the author of *Learning to Forgive, Putting Forgiveness into Practice,* and the forthcoming titles *Spiritual Exercises for Flabby Christians* and *Making Our Way through Conflict.*

VIRGIL ELIZONDO, founding president of the Mexican-American Cultural Center, is Rector of the Cathedral of San Fernando in San Antonio, Texas. A professor of Theology at Oblate School of Theology in San Antonio, he is the author of *Christianity and Culture* and *The Future is Mestizo: Life Where Cultures Meet.*

CAROL FRANCES JEGEN, BVM, is Professor of Religious Studies at Mundelein College in Chicago. A graduate of Marquette University, Dr. Jegen is the author of *Jesus the Peacemaker, Restoring Our Friendship with God,* and editor of *Mary According to Women.* She has served on the Advisory Board of the U.S. Catholic Bishops, the Board of Trustees of Catholic Theological Union, and the Board of Directors of the College Theology Society and of the Liturgical Conference.

ELIZABETH A. JOHNSON, CSJ, is Associate Professor of Theology at Catholic University of America, Washington, DC. She is a member of the Lutheran-Roman Catholic Dialogue (USA) which is presently completing its five-year dialogue round on Mary and the saints.

PHEME PERKINS, Professor of Theology (New Testament) at Boston College, has served as president of the Catholic Biblical Association. She is the author of fourteen books including *Reading the New Testament, The Resurrection, Hearing the Parables of Jesus, Love Commands in the New Testament, The Gnostic Dialogue,* and *Jesus as Teacher.*

DONALD SENIOR, CP, is Professor of New Testament and currently president of Catholic Theological Union in Chicago. He holds a doctorate in New Testament Studies from the University of Louvain, Belgium, and has written extensively on biblical topics.

JOHN R. SHINNERS is an associate professor teaching in the Humanistic Studies Program at Saint Mary's College, Notre Dame, Indiana. He earned his Ph.D. in Medieval Studies from the University of Toronto. His research focuses on medieval Christianity and he is currently working on a book about pastoral care in the middle ages.

RICHARD J. SKLBA, Auxiliary Bishop of Milwaukee, holds degrees from the Gregorian University (Rome), the Pontifical Biblical Institute (Rome) and the Angelicum (also in Rome). A former president of the Catholic Biblical Association of America, Bishop Sklba is the author of *The Faithful City* and *Words of Warning, Dreams of Hope.*